Darkened Waters

A Review of the History, Science, and Technology Associated with the *Exxon Valdez* Oil Spill and Cleanup

by Nancy Lord

A publication of the Homer Society of Natural History/Pratt Museum
to accompany the *Darkened Waters: Profile of an Oil Spill* exhibit

Copyright © 1992 by Homer Society of Natural History/Pratt Museum
3779 Bartlett Street, Homer, Alaska 99603

First Printing: 3,000 copies

This publication was produced by the Pratt Museum to accompany its exhibit, *Darkened Waters: Profile of an Oil Spill*. The author is responsible for all statements, whether of fact or opinion.

Lord, Nancy
    Darkened Waters: A Review of the History, Science, and Technology
    Associated with the *Exxon Valdez* Oil Spill and Cleanup. Homer, Alaska.
    Homer Society of Natural History/Pratt Museum, 1992
    Bibliography:
    1. Alaska. 2. Oil Spills I. Nancy Lord II. Homer Society of Natural
    History/Pratt Museum III. Title
ISBN no. 0-9619026-0-4

Design, typography and production:
Gordon Chun Design, Berkeley, California
    Gordon Chun
    Mary Jo Sutton
    Dana Nakagawa
    Suzanne Chun

Printing:
Worzalla Press, Stevens Point, Wisconsin

This publication was printed on recycled paper.

Cover: Oil-soaked cormorant in Prince William Sound.
Inset: The *Exxon Valdez* is towed off Bligh Reef.
Photos by Terrence McCarthy © 1992.

ABOUT THE AUTHOR

Nancy Lord is a writer who lives in Homer, Alaska. She is the author of two collections of short stories as well as numerous articles, essays, and reports. At the time of the *Exxon Valdez* oil spill, she was working as staff to the Alaska Legislature.

CONTENTS

We have accumulated knowledge of how cultures have shriveled and died, how species have been extinguished, and how our environment has been perilously damaged. It is now time to use this accumulated wisdom, born of loss, to help us heal, restore, and diversify further.

— Dr. Frank H. Talbot, Director
 National Museum of Natural History, Smithsonian Institution

UNIQUE IN THE EVOLUTIONARY HISTORY of the earth is the mass devastation of animal and plant life being brought about by man through the destruction of natural environments. One of the most menacing of all of our activities is the pollution of the world's oceans.

During the five centuries since Columbus's first contact, the diversity of New World peoples and their environment have suffered greatly. The need to understand these changes is stimulating a new awakening in the evolving role of museums. Specimen drawers and exhibitions of past life no longer satisfy the public mandate to preserve our rapidly diminishing natural and cultural heritage. In fact, collections have become a haunting record of what has been lost. As educational institutions, museums are now beginning to shift visitor focus from a state of passive curiosity to active involvement in important issues that concern human survival.

Homer, Alaska, and the Pratt Museum were deeply affected by the *Exxon Valdez* catastrophe. Now, three years after the event, we still have to wonder: what have we learned and are we better prepared today? The sights and odors of the massive death and destruction have moved into memory, assisted by time and the healing by natural processes.

The goal in creating the *Darkened Waters* traveling exhibition and this publication is to present our story to the public so that we, as a society, may find solutions to safe oil transportation and a more judicious use of petroleum in general. We naively began this project searching for the "truth," only to realize that there are many "truths." There are no easy answers, but surely clues are to be found through careful examination of the event. We have confidence in the public and sincerely believe that we can and must learn how to better protect our oceans. Through education and a willingness to become individually involved in these critical issues we may in time change our course.

Betsy Pitzman

Director, Pratt Museum
February 1992

ON MARCH 24, 1989, I awoke, along with the rest of Alaska, to radio news that a tanker had run aground on Bligh Reef in Prince William Sound. I recall now with embarrassment wondering if the millions of gallons of oil reported to be leaking was a large amount. Millions sounded like a lot, but I didn't have any reference points. My next thought was: surely they'll clean it up. I'd lived in Alaska since before the trans-Alaska pipeline was built, and I remembered the industry and government promises. There wouldn't be any big spills, but if there were, they'd be cleaned up right away.

The oil was not cleaned up—at least not very much of it, and not very quickly. Currents and storms moved it through and out of the sound, touching one community after another until eventually 1,244 miles of shoreline were oiled. Thousands of dead birds—many so coated with oil that they were unidentifiable—were collected, and sea otters were brought to emergency quarters in the Homer swimming pool. Commercial fisheries throughout the region were closed. One May day, exactly seven weeks after the *Exxon Valdez* grounding, pancakes of weathered oil began to wash up on our beach, some 400 miles from Bligh Reef.

We were all of us—Alaskans and Americans—to learn much more than we ever imagined about oil spills that year. The *Exxon Valdez*'s loss of nearly 11 million gallons of crude oil was the largest tanker spill ever in the United States and, arguably, the most destructive accidental spill to have occurred in the world. (The intentional Persian Gulf spill loosed 250 million gallons of oil into a shallow, low-energy marine system already faltering under the damage of previous spills.) A spill the size of that of the *Exxon Valdez*, we learned, is not containable or recoverable. We learned a new vocabulary: aromatic hydrocarbons, mousse (as emulsified oil), "pudding birds" (those unidentifiable birds coated in mousse), pom-poms (as a type of cleanup material), MACs (multi-agency coordinating groups), and bioremediation.

We were also shaken from our complacency. Oil spills do happen—catastrophically and chronically. Neither the oil industry nor government agencies are adequately prepared to deal with large spills. Americans have an enormous appetite for crude oil, and most of it is carried to us in a fleet of aging tankers. What can we do—what must we do—as communities and individuals, to prevent similar disasters from happening again?

At Homer's Pratt Museum, the board of directors and staff agreed that the museum should play a role in educating the public about the *Exxon Valdez* spill—what happened, what the scientific importance was, how people were affected by the crisis. The exhibit that was developed in Homer was well-received, with many visitors suggesting it be shared with people in other parts of the country. The traveling exhibit, *Darkened Waters: Profile of an Oil Spill,* was the result.

A recurring frustration in the development of both the original and traveling exhibits was the inability to address, in a presentation that was primarily visual, the background of the event and the sometimes complex science involved. There was no room to adequately discuss the ways in which oil enters the environment or the advantages and disadvantages of controversial cleaning technologies. Photographs could show oiled birds but couldn't explain which birds were most vulnerable, and why. This publication was designed to address in some greater depth—but certainly not in a definitive or comprehensive manner—some of the context and issues surrounding the *Exxon Valdez* oil spill.

Nancy Lord
November 1991

Oil flows for 786 miles through the 48-inch diameter trans-Alaska pipeline, from Prudhoe Bay to Valdez. Sections of the pipeline were built aboveground to prevent melting permafrost. The "fins" extending from the upright supports are part of a refrigeration system that helps keep the ground frozen.

©1992 KEN GRAHAM PHOTOGRAPHY

History—Oil in Alaska

ALASKA'S HISTORY AS AN OIL STATE dates back nearly a century, with lands along Cook Inlet drilled as early as 1898. An area of natural oil seeps just south of Cordova, on the Gulf of Alaska, was first drilled in 1902; ironically, the *Exxon Valdez* would spill its load of North Slope crude only miles from that early prospect.

In the 1920s President Harding set aside 25 million acres in Alaska's arctic for future oil exploration by the government. This expanse of natural seeps, first called Naval Petroleum Reserve No. 4, is today known as National Petroleum Reserve-Alaska, or NPRA.

The modern oil era began on the Kenai Peninsula south of Anchorage in 1957 with major strikes in the Kenai National Moose Range and, later, offshore in Cook Inlet. Anchorage and the Kenai area prospered, their economies fueled by oil industry support business and an influx of workers.

When Alaska became a state in 1959, it was widely acknowledged that the new state—with so much land mass and so few people—would need to depend on resource development to support itself. At statehood, Alaska was given 104 million acres of federal land as its own; it also was to continue receiving 90% of royalties from federal oil leases. Among Alaska's early land selections was the North Slope, where natural seeps and geological formations suggested likely oil and gas reserves—and near where the Navy had already discovered oil.

In 1968, Atlantic-Richfield (which later became ARCO) announced its Prudhoe Bay discovery—the largest oil field in North America. It was estimated to contain as much as 25 billion barrels of oil and another 30 trillion cubic feet of natural gas. Alaska sold leases to additional Prudhoe Bay tracts and began collecting—and spending—oil taxes and royalties. The state was on its way to becoming oil-dependent.

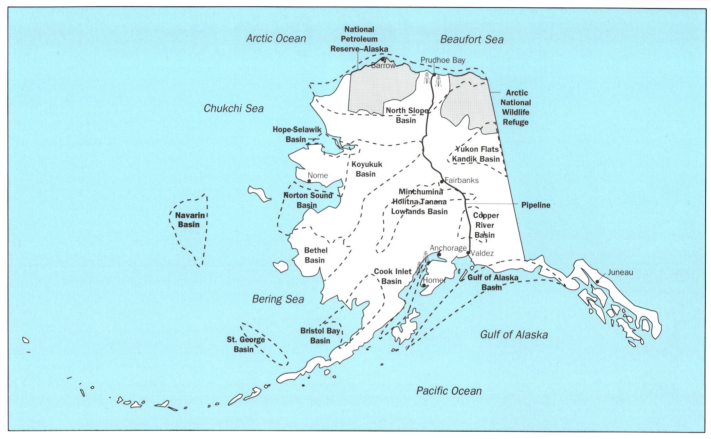

The dash-enclosed areas indicate basins with potential hydrocarbon formations; the potential for most is thought to be low. Today, most exploration and production occurs on the North Slope. The Cook Inlet fields, which have been declining since 1970, contribute only about 2% of the state's production. Oil industry interest is high in the coastal plain of the Arctic National Wildlife Refuge, an area now off-limits to drilling due to its wildlife and wilderness values.

The pipeline

The huge Prudhoe Bay field was a long way from the world's oil markets, and the oil industry quickly began planning a transportation system. Its suggested route was an 800-mile overland pipeline down the middle of the state to an ice-free port on the Gulf of Alaska, preferably at Valdez. This route was favored by the industry because of lower costs and shorter construction time, and a right-of-way application was formally filed with the U.S. Department of the Interior.

There were, however, numerous other ideas for transporting the oil. Some suggested shipping it through the Arctic Ocean all the way from the North Slope to east coast ports by ice-breaking or even submarine tankers. Others proposed a pipeline that would cross Alaska's northeast corner and continue through Canada to the Midwest. Supporters of the Canadian route included Canadians and Americans from northern states who liked the idea of oil being delivered directly to their markets. However, many Alaskans feared the Canadians would charge too much for transportation through their country, costs that would reduce the income to the state; they also argued that the Alaskan route would provide access to wider markets and better prices than would delivery to the Midwest alone. Alaskan labor unions lobbied for the Alaskan route to provide more jobs for Alaskans.

Environmental considerations were foremost in the opposition to the Alaskan route. Tanker safety was a major issue for the marine leg through Valdez Narrows and Prince William Sound, where icebergs and bad weather were common. Earthquakes were another concern, since a wave generated by a 1964 quake had destroyed the previous Valdez port and 325 homes.

A federal analysis concluded that the Alaskan route was preferable for cost and time reasons, as well as causing less environmental harm since it would cross—and thus disturb—less land than a Canadian route. The terrestrial damages were considered unavoidable, while damages to the marine environment from the tanker leg of the route were seen as only "potentials." Moreover, the analysis stated, the possibility of marine accidents could be mitigated by adopting strict standards for the tanker traffic.

Pipeline approval was not to come quickly, however. The new National Environmental Protection Act (NEPA) of 1969, which required an assessment of the social, economic, and environmental impacts of activities on federal lands, provided the grounds for a flurry of lawsuits. In addition, Alaskan Natives, whose land claims had been unresolved since Alaska's purchase from Russia in 1867, sued as the owners of land the pipeline would cross.

The Native claims were settled with relative speed, with the passage by Congress of the Alaska Native Claims Settlement Act in 1971. Newly created Native corporations received title to 44 million acres of land and $962 million.

The environmental issues were not solved so easily. Several million dollars were spent by government and the oil industry on ecological studies of the North Slope and pipeline cor-

ridor. In 1973 Congress voted to exempt the pipeline project from many of NEPA's environmental restrictions, with Vice President Spiro Agnew, acting as president of the Senate, casting the tie-breaking vote. Interior Secretary Rogers Morton promised Congress—and America—that protecting the environment would be a primary goal of the project. He assured those concerned about damage to Prince William Sound that tankers would have double bottoms and that sophisticated electronic equipment would be used to guarantee safe operations.

In the same authorization act, Congress stipulated that North Slope oil would be reserved for domestic use and not sold to foreign countries. The 82 million gallons of crude that would flow through the pipeline each day would account, in 1990, for roughly 25% of the nation's oil production and about 8% of its consumption.

Oil in transport

Pipeline construction under the management of Alyeska Pipeline Service Company (Alyeska), a consortium of seven oil companies, began in 1974, bringing a dramatic boom to Alaska—an influx of workers, large paychecks for many, social upheaval for others. The environmental studies forced by lawsuits resulted in the pipeline being engineered and constructed with considerable care for the environment; some portions were elevated to prevent the melting of permafrost, while others were buried to interfere as little as possible with wildlife crossings. By the time it was completed in 1977, the pipeline's cost had risen from the original $900 million estimate to $9 billion.

When the first oil was loaded into tankers at Valdez for its journey to the West Coast or Panama, double

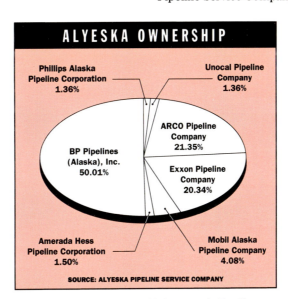

The major oil companies with interests in Prudhoe Bay joined together to form Alyeska Pipeline Service Company to build and operate the pipeline. Alyeska is responsible for oil spill contingency planning for the pipeline route, the Valdez port, and Prince William Sound.

bottoms were not required, and the Coast Guard had not installed either full-coverage radar or any other electronic surveillance in Prince William Sound. What they did have was a largely advisory system to monitor tankers through the Valdez Narrows, the most constricted passage in the sound, and to provide traffic and weather information. As the years passed, budget cuts and complacency reduced even this level of oversight.

The State of Alaska initially tried to strengthen its regulation of shipping safety with passage of a 1976 law giving it broad authority to regulate tanker traffic in state waters and to provide incentives for improved safety measures. The oil industry challenged the law on grounds that it preempted federal authority,

and after a district court ruling in the industry's favor, the legislature repealed the act. Alaska never would become much of an oil industry regulator; it resigned itself, for the most part, to be a tax collector. Today, 85% of the state's revenues come from oil taxes and royalties, and all Alaskans receive a yearly dividend check (nearly $1000 in recent years) as "shareholders" in an oil-rich state.

By the early 1980s, the oil shipping industry was in a slump. Cost-cutting measures resulted in steadily decreasing crew sizes, more reliance on automation, and continual pressure to meet deadlines. Alyeska resisted recommendations from both the Coast Guard and the state to strengthen its cleanup capability, and the adequacy of its contingency plans was repeatedly

In 1989 one old tanker, surrounded by boom as it loaded in Valdez, leaked so much that the oil overwhelmed the boom and spilled 72,000 gallons at the port.

In June of 1987 the *Glacier Bay,* a tanker carrying North Slope crude from the Valdez terminal to a refinery in Cook Inlet, hit a rock in upper Cook Inlet and spilled 125,000 gallons of oil. This was Alaska's first oil spill to seriously jeopardize marine resources and the livelihoods of Alaskans, and it was apparent that there was not an adequate plan to contain or recover the oil. Swift tides quickly carried the crude through the inlet and mixed it into tidal rips where it was difficult to recover among mats of sticks and other debris. The opening of the commercial salmon season was delayed for fear of contaminated nets and fish. Only 15% of the oil was ever recovered. The spill resulted in numerous lawsuits over financial damages but no real changes in tanker transport procedures or contingency planning.

For 12 years, tanker traffic in Prince William Sound failed to raise many concerns. Tankers loaded with crude—an average of two each day—made more than 8700 passages through the sound between 1977 and 1989. In the Port Valdez and Prince William Sound area, 440 mostly minor spills were reported. There were also a few "close calls" such as the occasion when, in 1980, a fully-loaded tanker lost power in high winds and drifted out of control for 17 hours. Then the single-hulled *Exxon Valdez*, Exxon's newest and most advanced tanker, drove onto Bligh Reef. ■

called into question. When the state forced Alyeska, in 1986, to include in its plan a scenario for a 200,000-barrel spill (8.4 million gallons), it protested that such a spill could only be expected to happen once every 241 years.

Other cost-cutting measures in the industry involved putting off purchases of new tankers. On average, tankers used to transport Alaskan crude across the Gulf of Alaska—the roughest water crossed by any U.S. ships—are 15 years older than the rest of the U.S. fleet. An analysis released in 1988 found that the rate of structural failure among tankers traveling Alaskan waters was unusually high. Although tankers of the Alaskan fleet represented only one-eighth of the ships surveyed, they had more than half the cracks and other structural failures.

Crude Oil in the Sea

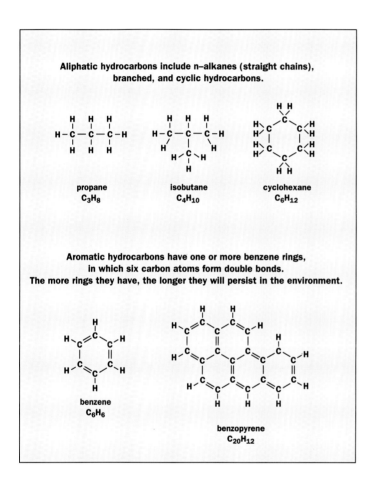

Aliphatic hydrocarbons include n–alkanes (straight chains), branched, and cyclic hydrocarbons.

propane
C_3H_8

isobutane
C_4H_{10}

cyclohexane
C_6H_{12}

Aromatic hydrocarbons have one or more benzene rings, in which six carbon atoms form double bonds. The more rings they have, the longer they will persist in the environment.

benzene
C_6H_6

benzopyrene
$C_{20}H_{12}$

In ten days, wind, waves, and currents had spread oil from the Exxon Valdez *over 1000 square miles. Here, in a bay on Eleanor Island in Prince William Sound, the oil was a foot thick.*

POLLUTION OF THE OCEAN by oil is a worldwide problem that increases with the accelerated development of offshore petroleum reserves and expanded oil tanker traffic. While the immediate, catastrophic effects of a spill are apparent in terms of oiled birds and blackened shorelines, the fate of oil in the marine environment is, despite many studies, imperfectly understood. Exact knowledge of the disposition of oil and its degraded components after a spill is impossible to attain, but efforts can be made to understand the processes involved. A first step is to understand what oil is, how it enters the sea, and something about the complex interactions that take place once it's in the marine environment.

What is oil?

Crude oil is a complex mixture of organic (carbon-based) and inorganic (noncarbon-based) compounds. Hydrocarbons, which make up the bulk of crude oil, are simply organic compounds composed of hydrogen and carbon. The inorganic components of crude include sulfur, oxygen, nitrogen, and trace metals. Every type of crude, depending on its place of origin and even its location within a given geological formation, has its own unique mix of hydrocarbons and other compounds. In fact, when a mysterious spill occurs at sea, tests can identify the source—the tanker and load—much as a fingerprint can identify a person.

Hydrocarbons fall into two groups, or fractions, depending on their molecular structures: aliphatic (or paraffinic) and aromatic. The aromatic hydrocarbons (so named because they usually have a strong odor) are more toxic than the aliphatics. While the molecules in aliphatic hydrocarbons occur in open chains, the aromatic hydrocarbons include one or more benzene rings, hexagonal structures that fit together like chickenwire. Of the aromatics, those with low molecular weights (fewer rings) have the greatest immediate toxicity because they are easily water soluble. Those with high molecu-lar weights (more rings) are less water soluble and thus take longer to break down in the environment. Their persistency means that they remain in the environment longer and thus act as slower poisons. Some high-weight aromatics are known to induce cancer.

North Slope crude, such as that spilled by the *Exxon Valdez*, contains a high proportion of aromatic hydrocarbons and a wide variety of sulfur compounds. It is more toxic than crudes that contain fewer aromatics. Compared to the crudes of California, for example, North Slope crude is highly toxic.

The refining process involves heating and distilling crude oil until the compounds, based on their different boiling points, are separated or "cracked." Subsequent blending results in a wide variety of petroleum products. Gasoline, for example, is a light distillate, which means that, while it's highly toxic, a spill of gasoline largely evaporates. Fuel oil is the heaviest distillate and will take longer than other distillates to break down in the environment, but not as long as crude oil. Asphalt is a non-volatile solid with high molecular weights and will persist in the environment for a very long time.

How does oil get into the ocean?

Ever since its first formation in geological time, oil has been coming to the surface of the earth through fissures in its crust. Such oil was not regarded as pollution, and there are numerous accounts of it being collected and used for various purposes. Paleolithic cultures used natural tar to attach spear points to shafts, and Arabian and Syrian tribesmen fought in Biblical times over asphalt slabs that floated up from the bottom of the Dead Sea. Since the earliest times, mariners poured oil on water to calm the surface; Aristotle told of ancient Greek sponge divers who released oil from their mouths to smooth the ripples above and give them better light.

However, just in the last hundred years, human-caused escapes of oil into the environment have greatly increased in quantity and caused serious pollution problems. A pollutant, by defi-nition, is any substance—even a naturally occurring one—that's

added to the environment in amounts sufficient to cause biological effects.

At every stage of its production, transport, refining, and use, oil can escape and enter the environment. Oil wells blow out of control, tankers have accidents or discharge oily ballast water, storage tanks leak, refineries and petrochemical plants discharge effluent, pipelines break. Ordinary industrial and domestic sewage inevitably contains automotive and other oily waste. Storm drains carry petroleum products to the sea, from street runoff after rains. Even after oil has been burned for fuel, gases containing unburned hydrocarbons wash from the air into the sea.

Exact amounts are difficult to track, but 1985 estimates by the National Academy of Science suggest that, globally, between 1.7 and 8.8 million metric tons of oil from all sources enter the sea each year, with a best estimate of 3.25 million metric tons. Converted to gallons, that's a best estimate of 960 million gallons of oil entering the oceans each year.

Of this, the largest amount, 45%, is estimated to come from transportation activities. Roughly half of that comes from tanker

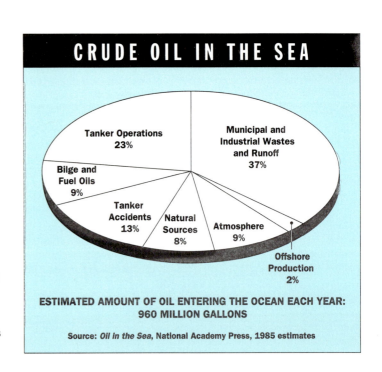

CRUDE OIL IN THE SEA

Tanker Operations 23%

Bilge and Fuel Oils 9%

Tanker Accidents 13%

Natural Sources 8%

Municipal and Industrial Wastes and Runoff 37%

Atmosphere 9%

Offshore Production 2%

ESTIMATED AMOUNT OF OIL ENTERING THE OCEAN EACH YEAR: 960 MILLION GALLONS

Source: *Oil in the Sea*, National Academy Press, 1985 estimates

operations, a quarter from bilge and fuel oils, and a quarter from tanker accidents. Much smaller amounts come from dry-docking, terminals, and nontanker accidents.

To put that another way, twice as much oil enters the sea from normal tanker operations as from accidents such as groundings. When a tanker unloads its crude at a terminal, sea water is routinely loaded into its tanks for stability, or ballast. Until quite recently, the small amount of oil left in the tanks—perhaps 0.3% of the total volume of oil—was mixed with the water and later dumped at sea before the tanker reloaded. Today, most nations prohibit intentional discharge of such wastes. Enforcement, however, is very difficult on the open ocean, and the practice continues. The use of "top loading" (separation of dirty ballast water into a single slop tank, which is eventually mixed with new oil and unloaded at a refinery), segregated ballast tanks, and on-shore ballast treatment plants have reduced the amount of oil entering the oceans through tanker operations, but it is still a major source of oil pollution.

Notably, nearly as much oil, 37% of the total, enters the sea from municipal and industrial wastes and runoff as from transportation. A large source of this is automotive: leaking gas tanks and, especially, waste oil.

Smaller amounts of oil enter the sea from the atmosphere (9%), natural sources (8%), and offshore production (2%).

Natural seeps

Oil enters the environment naturally in two ways: through erosional processes and natural seeps. The amount contributed through erosion of exposed oil-bearing sedimentary rocks is thought to be minor. Natural seeps—particularly submarine ones—are, however, a significant source of oil in the environment.

The asphalt lakes of Trinidad are one example of a giant seep, and it's been suggested that the pillar of fire that led Moses and the Israelites to the Promised Land may have been a seep burning in the desert. Such seeps are generally associated with geologically active areas such as the southern coast of Alaska and the area off the coast of California. Among the most prolific

Natural seeps like this one near Cape Yakataga on Alaska's southern coast alerted prospectors a century ago to Alaska's oil potential.

are those in California's Santa Barbara Channel, where one seep (at Coal Oil Point) released 2500 gallons of oil per day during a study period. Tar balls frequently collect on nearby beaches.

In areas of natural seeps, some plants and animals have evolved to coexist with oil and beach tar. It has been suggested—but not scientifically determined—that the relatively rapid biological recovery following the 1969 Santa Barbara offshore oil rig blowout may have been assisted by the adaptation of many local organisms to a certain amount of chronic oil pollution.

Spilled oil spreads out on the surface of water. Here, sunlight reflects off a portion of the Exxon Valdez *slick, 40 miles from the wrecked tanker.*

©1992 TERRENCE MCCARTHY

When oil enters water

Once crude oil enters the ocean, it immediately begins to weather. Weathering consists of various processes, including spreading, evaporation, dissolution, dispersion, emulsification, and photochemical oxidation. Some oil will stick to suspended particulate matter and sink. Some will be ingested by microbes and other organisms. Through all these processes, the oil is not "disappearing" but is being partitioned, its components transferred into the environment.

Exactly how a given sample of oil reacts in the water depends on many factors, including the type and dose of oil spilled, the temperature and condition of the water, the types and numbers of plants and animals in the area, and previous exposure of the area to oil or other pollutants. The natural processes are speeded by wind, waves, and currents that increase spreading and vertical mixing. Various fractions (aromatic versus aliphatic hydrocarbons, for example) respond differently, and weathered oil behaves differently than freshly spilled oil.

Evaporation and dissolution occur relatively quickly, in the first hours or days of a spill. The low molecular weight aromatic hydrocarbons (known as the "light ends") evaporate off the water's surface into the atmosphere. The rate of evaporation loss depends on the proportion of light ends in the oil, with most evaporation occurring within the first 48 hours after a spill. Dissolution, or transfer of hydrocarbons into the water column, involves a relatively small percentage of the oil mass.

While evaporation and dissolution describe molecular transfer, dispersion describes the transfer of discrete oil droplets into the water column. Because these droplets resemble the parent oil in composition, they can carry toxic hydrocarbons to organisms that feed below the water's surface.

With the light end hydrocarbons evaporated or dissolved, the aliphatics and the higher weight aromatics are left behind. Thus, the oil mass remaining in the water is more viscous:

it's heavier and stickier. The aliphatics are quite easily broken down or metabolized by bacteria or other organisms in a process known as biodegradation. The higher weight aromatics can also be metabolized in this same process, but over a longer period of time. Complete biological oxidation of oil by microorganisms results in mineralization—the formation of carbon dioxide, water, sulphates, and nitrates as major products—but many of the biological reactions do not go to completion. Intermediate products of the reactions—such as acids, aldehydes, ketones, alcohols, peroxides, and sulfoxides—may dissolve into the water or be deposited in sediments, to remain

Wind can whip oil into a frothy brown emulsion called "mousse." The smooth area here is a thick mousse layer floating on water.

©1992 KEN GRAHAM PHOTOGRAPHY

Viscous weathered oil will mix with sediments and sink or wash up on beaches as tar balls.

©1992 KEN GRAHAM PHOTOGRAPHY

in the environment for a very long time. Some of these intermediate products are harmless and some are toxic or mutagenic.

Rough seas tend to mix water into the oil to form a water-in-oil emulsion or "mousse," so named because of its resemblance to chocolate pudding. Mousse can contain up to 70 or 80% water, which means that a mass of spilled oil can seemingly multiply as it emulsifies. When mousse forms, the oil in the emulsion is less exposed to air and thus will evaporate much more slowly. Bacterial action, which requires oxygen, is greatly slowed down as well. Mousse is, therefore, much more stable in the marine environment than the original crude oil. Because its density is lighter than water, it accumulates in thick layers on the surface. With time, it will eventually break apart and form tar balls. When mousse washes ashore, it tends to thoroughly coat and smother entire beaches and communities of organisms.

Oil also changes chemically with exposure to light—a poorly understood process known as photochemical oxidation. In some cases, this process results in greater toxicity.

Sinking of oil takes place when its density becomes greater than water, by adherence to suspended sediments that carry oil to the bottom, or when, after being weathered, it solidifies into tar balls or asphalt. In the case of the Santa Barbara blowout, a flood shortly afterward carried sediments into the ocean; oil

clung to these suspended particles and resulted in much of it being carried to the sea floor. However, glacial silt in Alaska's Cook Inlet has had no apparent effect in sinking the crude oil of that region. Oil or its degraded products that sink to the bottom might be trapped in sediments for a very long time but can eventually be ingested and further biodegraded by organisms that live on the sea floor.

The rate at which oil weathers depends on temperature. The degradation by microbes is temperature dependent, with generally less activity at colder temperatures. Moreover, evaporation is slower at colder temperatures, which means that the aromatic hydrocarbons remain with the oil for a longer time—slowing microbial growth as well as posing more hazard to all organisms with which they come in contact.

Final fates

Oil in the sea ends up, finally, partitioned into places and forms that make it much less obvious than an initial slick. Although there are few good measurement tools to track oil through the environment, it's possible to make some rough estimates.

In 1978 the *Amoco Cadiz* grounded off the coast of France and spilled 70 million gallons of light Arabian and Iranian crude oils. Some limited chemical dispersants were used to try to break up the oil before it hit shore. Estimates are that approximately 30% of the oil evaporated, 14% rapidly dispersed into the water column, 8% was deposited in subtidal sediments, and 28% washed ashore. The remaining 20% is unaccounted for. Of the oil that washed ashore, approximately 40% was collected by cleanup workers. The oil that dispersed into the water column must later have partitioned further through evaporation and dissolution, been biodegraded, or deposited in sediments. Oil in sediments or on shore eventually biodegrades as well, but today there are still asphalt-based substances on French beaches.

Estimates of what happened to the oil spilled from the *Exxon Valdez* have covered a wide range. Previous tests of North Slope crude suggested that 15–20% of the oil would evaporate, but other scientists estimated that as much as 30–40% of the spill

ERIC GUNDLACH

The Amoco Cadiz *grounded in 1978 off the coast of France and spilled six times as much crude oil as the* Exxon Valdez.

evaporated. A very small amount—15,000 gallons—was burned. Perhaps 58% of the spilled oil reached shore. The total amount recovered by Exxon's two billion dollar cleanup effort was estimated by the U.S. Environmental Protection Agency at 23%, by an independent state commission at less than 10%, and by the Alaska Department of Environmental Conservation at 8%. The unrecovered and unaccounted for portions of the oil remain in the water or on the sea floor, in bottom or beach sediments, in organisms, and as metabolized products of biodegradation. ■

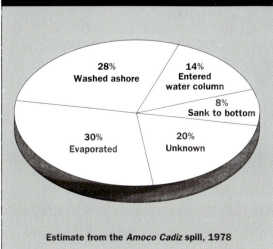

Final Fate of Oil from *Amoco Cadiz*

28% Washed ashore

14% Entered water column

8% Sank to bottom

30% Evaporated

20% Unknown

Estimate from the *Amoco Cadiz* spill, 1978

Oil in the Food Web—Biological Effects

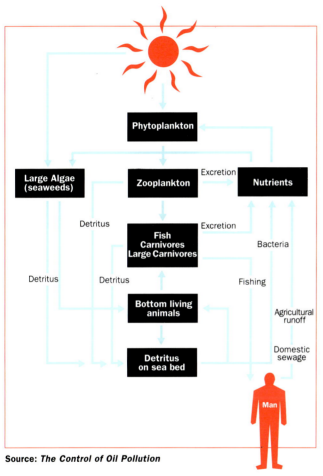

Source: *The Control of Oil Pollution*

Oil and its components pass through the marine food web and circulate in the environment as organisms feed on one another, excrete wastes, and die.

This brown bear has a patch of oiled fur. Terrestrial mammals such as black and brown bears, foxes, mink, deer, and river otters are exposed to oil when they forage on oiled beaches and feed on oiled carcasses or vegetation. They can also absorb oil through their skin and through respiration. Preliminary studies of brown bear fecal samples and tissues after the Exxon Valdez *spill showed some exposure to petroleum hydrocarbons, but no conclusive injury has been documented.*

WHEN AN OIL SPILL OCCURS, the effects on certain birds and marine mammals are immediate and obvious. Not so obvious are the effects on less visible parts of the food web and on individual biological processes. Damage to species populations such as phytoplankton at the base of the food web can affect the entire ecosystem over a long period of time. Sublethal effects on individuals—because all repair and recovery requires energy—can result in increased vulnerability to disease or to decreased growth rate and reproductive success. Chronic and sublethal effects of oil at the biological community level are not understood very well, and many after-the-fact studies are of limited use because so little was known of pre-spill conditions.

It must be stressed that, in the case of the *Exxon Valdez* spill, relatively little baseline knowledge was available against which to compare conditions after the spill. In addition, the results of most of the scientific studies conducted after the spill had not been released by Exxon or the state and federal governments by late 1991.

There is some evidence that invertebrates, fish, seabirds, and marine mammals can avoid polluted waters. However, even when an animal successfully avoids oil, it is not necessarily responding in a manner that leads to survival. In the process of avoiding oil, other critical resources such as food and shelter may be lost. For example, clams have been shown to remain closer to the surface in oiled sediments to avoid deeper oiled sediments. As a result, they are more susceptible to predation.

Effects on biological processes

Both plants and animals—through contact with oil and in the process of breaking it down and ridding themselves of it—can encounter problems in development, metabolism, respiration, growth, reproduction, and behavior.

Damage by oil to chromosomes or chromosome functions is

poorly understood, and research on oil-induced aberrations in marine organisms is limited. Evidence exists, however, that chromosome mutation does occur, at least in marine invertebrates and fish, particularly in embryonic and juvenile stages. Increased mutation reduces the genetic fitness of both individuals and populations. Species that reproduce often and in high numbers are less affected than those with slower reproduction times and fewer offspring.

Hydrocarbons can cause the gonads of some species to develop abnormally and can cause the delayed and deformed development of embryos and larvae. The hatching success of both fish and birds is impeded by exposure to hydrocarbons.

Feeding in most species exposed to hydrocarbons is reduced; the consequences are most serious in species with little food reserves (fat) and short life cycles. Depression of respiration has been observed in a range of marine organisms similarly exposed, including crustaceans, molluscs, and fish. Growth, too, is markedly affected in a variety of organisms; particularly susceptible are bottom-dwellers such as molluscs and flatfish that are in direct contact with oiled sediments.

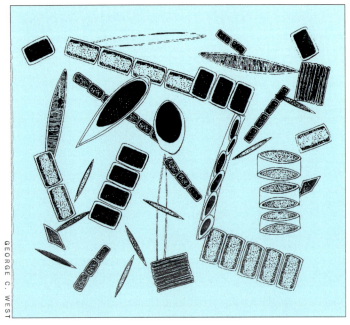

GEORGE C. WEST

Phytoplankton, here drawn as they appear under a microscope, cannot be seen unless magnified many times.

Less is known about the interaction of hydrocarbons with the more fundamental processes of animal metabolism such as enzyme activity and ion transport. It is well known that one enzyme, cytochrome P-450E, is produced by fish in the presence of oil. Its role is to catalyze certain reactions in the metabolism of hydrocarbons. This enzyme's action can also result in the production of carcinogenic and mutagenic compounds, leading to adverse effects in both general health and reproductive abilities.

In plants, two areas of metabolism that can be upset by oil are photosynthesis (the use of sunlight to convert carbon dioxide and water into complex organic materials) and cellular activity. For example, the microscopic marine plants known as phytoplankton have widely varying responses to oil, sometimes showing enhanced photosynthesis and sometimes inhibited processes. Some algae exposed to oil have exhibited disruptions in cellular activity, including cellular "leakage" and disruption of DNA synthesis. Abnormal growth of some plants has also been documented.

Chemoreception, or an animal's use of chemical senses in feeding, reproduction, habitat selection, or predator recognition—is easily altered by exposure to oil. Studies have shown, for example, that the chemoreception of crabs and lobsters, through their antennae, is impaired by hydrocarbons. Oil can similarly interfere with sex pheromone production and recognition in some species; that is, the chemicals released by organisms to attract members of the opposite sex by smell can be blocked or go unrecognized, leading to less successful breeding.

Effects on microorganisms and plankton

The effect of oil on marine microorganisms depends on the type and amount of oil spilled, the physical nature of the area, nutritional status, oxygen concentration, and the area's previous exposure to hydrocarbons. Prior exposure will influence the number and types of microorganisms present, as well as their metabolic ability to process hydrocarbons. Thus, in waters affected by chronic oil pollution, at least some of the microorganisms present will have the ability to consume hydrocarbons to grow and increase in numbers, while in an

Plants growing in intertidal areas are very vulnerable to oil and cleanup activities, but populations also appear to recover quite readily. These, known as Fucus *or rockweed, are the dominant intertidal plants in Prince William Sound; their numbers, size, and reproduction were greatly reduced following the* Exxon Valdez *spill. Note the contrast between the photographs of clean (above) and oiled (left) rockweed.*

unpolluted area most microorganisms will be killed or have their growth suppressed. In chronically oil polluted ecosystems, the majority of microorganisms may be hydrocarbon utilizers, while in unpolluted ecosystems, such utilizers generally constitute less than one-tenth of 1%. In some unpolluted ecosystems, however, there exist hydrocarbons—called terpenes—produced by living plants, and the microorganisms that feed on them will also be able to metabolize some of the hydrocarbons found in crude oil.

Phytoplankton, those tiny plants that live in sunlit surface waters, are one of the most important life forms in the ocean; they produce through photosynthesis nearly 80% of the world's oxygen and form the principal basis of the food web. At high enough concentrations, oil can upset phytoplankton photosynthesis or kill the plants outright. Growth is generally retarded by oil but is very dependent on the dose, and very low concentrations of some oils have been shown to actually stimulate growth. It is not well known how phytoplankton specifically respond to a spill. Because regeneration times are very fast and plankton can quickly move in from adjacent waters, the long-term effects of oil on phytoplankton are probably negligible. In one case, shortly after a spill phytoplankton populations were found to be higher than usual; this is probably because the oil had reduced the population of zooplankton, which feed on phytoplankton.

Zooplankton include not only the tiny animals that spend their entire lives drifting or swimming near the ocean's surface, but also others that spend only the early stages of their lives there before maturing into bottom-dwelling adults. The larvae of barnacles, worms, clams, and crabs are all zooplankton, as are jellyfish, which can grow to six feet in diameter. Zooplankton are the basic food of many other marine animals, from clams to whales. They are highly vulnerable to dispersed and dissolved oil, although their capabilities to metabolize and detoxify hydrocarbons vary. Studies have detected adverse biological effects from both oil spills and chronic pollution, but these changes are generally short-lived since—like phytoplankton—zooplankton are widely distributed and populations regenerate rapidly. Individual organisms are affected in a number of ways: direct mortality, external contamination, tissue contamination, abnormal development of embryos, inhibition of feeding, and altered metabolic rates. Zooplankton are most vulnerable to oil during reproductive periods and in their embryonic and larval stages.

Effects on intertidal and subtidal plants

Little is known about the effect of oil on most plants. Biological processes can certainly be disrupted, as noted above. On the community scale, plants growing in intertidal areas are very vulnerable to oiling by spills that reach shore, but they also appear to recover quite readily. Subtidal or submerged plants are perhaps somewhat less vulnerable to oiling, depending on the depth of the water. The impact of oil on marine plants depends on the amount and type of oil present and the local mixing conditions. A few species of algae have been observed to actually flourish after a spill, but this was a result of the elimination by oil of intertidal herbivores such as limpets.

Effects on intertidal and benthic invertebrates

Considerable study had been made of the effects of oil on some intertidal and benthic (bottom dwelling) species, particularly those with economic value, such as clams, crabs, and lobsters. Generalizations are difficult, however, because of differences among species and even among the various life-cycle stages of a given species. Juvenile and molting stages tend to be most vulnerable. Species such as barnacles and limpets that attach themselves can be smothered by oil; oil can also cause them to loosen their hold so that they fall free and become vulnerable to

©1992 KAREN JETTMAR

The sea star here has been coated with oil. Such oiling may immediately affect its feeding and mobility.

predators. More mobile invertebrates can be immobilized and thus made more susceptible to toxic effects or predators.

Offshore benthic species are initially protected from an oil spill by the intervening water column. However, as oil dissolves, disperses, and is deposited in sediments, these species, too, are vulnerable, on both the individual and community levels.

Invertebrates can be killed outright by oil or can suffer sublethal effects including genetic alteration, suppressed reproduction, metabolic and feeding problems, reduced filtration rates, restricted growth, and changes in shell formation.

Effects on fish

Fish can ingest oil or take up dissolved compounds through their gills, or their eggs can be coated. In general, some stages of egg development and most stages of larvae are more vulnerable to oil than are juveniles and adults. An exception is salmon eggs, which appear to be quite tolerant. Damage to an embryo is often not apparent until it hatches. Many larvae hatched from eggs exposed to oil are found to be deformed and incapable of swimming.

Fish have the ability to metabolize hydrocarbons to some extent, and they can excrete both parent hydrocarbons and metabolites (products of metabolism) from the gills and liver. In fish, oil can cause damage to the liver, gills, eye lens, stomach, brain, gonads, and olfactory organs. Physiological changes can include increased heart rate, ionic and osmotic imbalances, changes in respiration, decreased energy reserves, and changes in gill enzymes.

There is some evidence that fish will avoid oil. In one study of adult salmon returning to a home stream, about half avoided a contaminated fish ladder. Other fish have, in the presence of oil, lost their normal schooling behavior, perhaps because of damaged or blocked olfactory organs. In other cases, fish have been attracted to oiled areas because of the availability of easy prey.

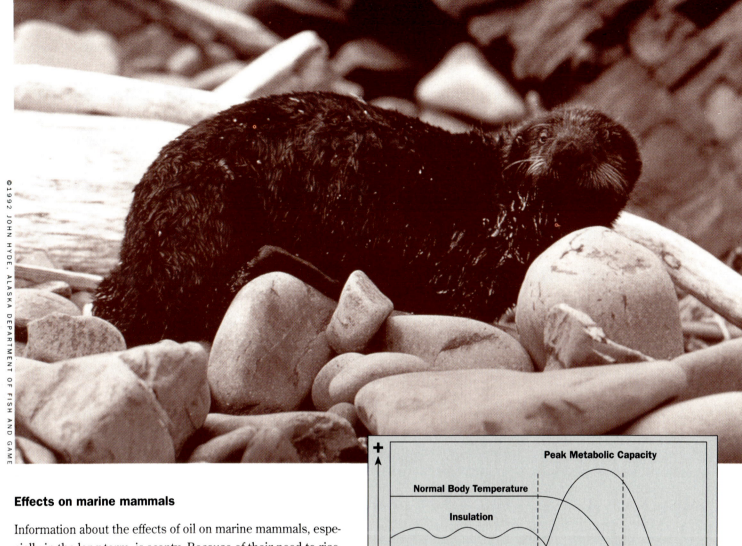

©1992 JOHN HYDE, ALASKA DEPARTMENT OF FISH AND GAME

GEORGE C. WEST

Graph labels:
+
Peak Metabolic Capacity
Normal Body Temperature
Insulation
Metabolism
−
Oil Contaminates Fur or Feathers   Hypothermia   Death

Effects on marine mammals

Information about the effects of oil on marine mammals, especially in the long-term, is scanty. Because of their need to rise through the surface of the water to breathe, marine mammals are vulnerable to direct oiling. Those animals that groom their coats are additionally vulnerable to the ingestion of oil. Most species do not appear to avoid oil-contaminated waters.

Marine mammals that ingest oil, through grooming or the eating of oiled foods, metabolize it and excrete the petroleum residues and metabolites. Seals and sea otters have been shown to accumulate petroleum residues in their livers. Polar bears have been found with high hydrocarbon levels in their kidneys, brains, and bone marrow; large doses lead to kidney failure. Oiling can also damage the skin and eyes. Inhaling oil fumes can cause lung damage including emphysema.

The sea otter is particularly vulnerable to coating by oil since it relies on its thick, water-repellent fur and the air trapped within it for warmth. Unlike most marine mammals, which have layers of blubber to keep them warm, otters have very little body fat.

Top: *Oiled otters suffer both from the cold and from ingesting oil as they try to clean their coats. This one has apparently left the frigid water in an attempt to keep warm.*

Bottom: *Birds and mammals maintain body temperature by a combination of insulation and metabolic heat production. When oiling causes a decrease in the insulating qualities of plumage or fur, metabolism must increase to compensate. If peak metabolic capacity cannot produce enough heat to maintain body temperature, hypothermia occurs and will result in death.*

Oiled birds like this loon die from hypothermia, drowning, and the toxic effects of oil ingested during preening and feeding.

gastrointestinal tract, as well as a reduction in white blood cells and a loss of fat and muscle tissues.

Relatively small amounts of ingested oil can cause a temporary depression of egg laying and reduces the hatching success of eggs that are laid.

The birds most susceptible to oil pollution are those that gather in groups, spend most of their time on the water, and dive rather than fly up when disturbed. Alcids, including murres, are especially vulnerable and have already suffered serious declines worldwide partly due to oil pollution. Their reproductive strategy, designed to cope with erratic natural conditions such as fluctuations in their food supply, is a low reproductive rate combined with longevity. Diving duck populations are somewhat less sensitive to oiling because of a breeding strategy that involves higher reproductive rates.

Their fur consists of an outer layer of guard hairs over a very dense layer of underfur—the densest of any animal, with 675,000 hairs per square inch. Oiling reduces the insulation value of the fur and requires the animal to compensate by increasing its metabolism to generate more body heat. If an increase in metabolism can't compensate for heat loss, then the animal will die from hypothermia (low body temperature).

Effects on birds

Birds are the most obvious casualties of marine oil pollution. The direct effect of oil on an individual bird is to clog the fine structure of its feathers, which are responsible—like an otter's fur—for maintaining water repellency and heat insulation. Oiled plumage absorbs water and the bird sinks and drowns. The loss of insulation results in increased metabolic activity to maintain body temperature. Fat and muscle reserves are rapidly exhausted, leading to death from hypothermia. Birds in cold climates or in situations where their energy reserves are low are more likely to succumb to oiling than birds in warmer climates or with higher energy reserves.

Although the major cause of bird deaths by oiling is drowning or hypothermia, birds that ingest oil through preening and feeding show abnormal conditions in the lungs, kidneys, liver, and

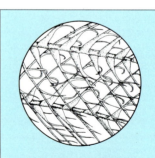

A normal, clean feather (here magnified several hundred times) is made up of barbs that branch into a network of smaller barbs. Tiny hooklets hold the feather together and surround microscopic air spaces that serve as insulation.

When oil is absorbed by a feather, the barbs are drawn together in clumps, oil fills gaps, and the air spaces and their insulation value are lost.

©1992 TERRENCE MCCARTHY

GEORGE C. WEST

Effects on humans

Humans can be exposed to hydrocarbons in the environment either through direct contact or, as a member of the food web, from contaminated foods. Acute exposure can come from inhalation, skin contact, or by the direct ingestion of oil or its products. The limited information available on the metabolism of hydrocarbons by humans suggests that most compounds are readily metabolized and do not tend to accumulate in the body. A few hydrocarbon compounds, including benzene, are known to be human carcinogens, but amounts obtained from foods are considered negligible.

Oil cleanup workers are exposed to hydrocarbons through skin contact and inhalation of fumes. Exposure can cause headaches, nausea, and skin rashes.

The *Exxon Valdez* spill—a preliminary assessment of effects

The *Exxon Valdez* oil spill occurred at a particularly sensitive time of year in southcentral Alaska. In late March, phytoplankton and zooplankton were just beginning their annual bloom. Salmon fry were emerging from gravel beds and hatcheries to feed on that bloom. During the two months after the spill major migrations of salmon and birds passed through oiled areas, and the reproductive periods for most species of marine life took place while the oil was in its most concentrated and damaging forms.

Exxon and the state and federal governments embarked on millions of dollars worth of spill-related studies to try to determine short- and long-term damages to the ecosystem. These were considered "litigation sensitive" and were held in secrecy until, two years after the spill, the federal government released a 15-page "Summary of Effects," drawn from work done for both it and the State of Alaska. Aside from this slim report, which emphasizes the preliminary nature of its findings, almost no scientific information had been made available to the public by late 1991.

Perhaps 10% of the murres in the Gulf of Alaska were killed by the Exxon Valdez *spill; after the spill, colonies in the area suffered complete reproductive failure.*

The federal summary reported significant and pervasive short-term damage to individual marine organisms and entire populations. It also noted that latent or sublethal effects on reproductive and other systems might not become fully evident for many years.

The number of birds estimated to have been killed by the spill was 260,000 to 580,000. Of those, 172,000 to 198,000 were

Murres are among the birds most vulnerable to oil spills and have suffered serious declines worldwide partly due to oil pollution.

Eagles encounter oil when they feed on oiled prey. Even small amounts of ingested oil can depress egg laying and reduce the hatching success of eggs that are laid.

murres, which mature and breed slowly, laying only one egg per year. Overall, perhaps 10% of the murres in the Gulf of Alaska were killed, with some colonies losing up to 70% of their members. Moreover, the colonies in the spill area had complete reproductive failure in both 1989 and 1990, with a lost production of at least 215,000 chicks. One researcher estimated that it could take up to 70 years for the hardest hit colonies to recover.

Other birds hit hard included pigeon guillemots, which lost 10% of their total Gulf of Alaska population, and harlequin ducks, sea ducks that feed in the shallow intertidal zone and that failed to reproduce in 1990. After the spill 144 bald eagles were found dead, and several times that number are thought to have been killed and not found. In 1989 85% of eagle nests in moderately to heavily oiled areas did not produce young. The extent of injury to many other bird species—including loons, grebes, cormorants, gulls, auklets, murrelets, and puffins—will probably never be known because pre-spill information on their numbers did not exist.

Among marine mammals, studies confirmed that sea otters were particularly vulnerable to the spill. Out of a total area population of 20,000, 3500 to 5500 sea otters were estimated to have been killed directly by the spill. Some of these died from hypothermia after their fur lost its insulating qualities, but others died from inhaling toxic fumes and from ingesting oil as they tried to clean their coats by grooming. Otters continued to be injured after the spill through feeding on contaminated sea urchins and clams. Analyses of blood and fat samples in 1990 showed elevated concentrations of hydrocarbons; carcasses of animals in the prime of life continued to be found a year and more after the spill, and reproduction rates remained low.

Other mammals were also harmed by the spill. Two hundred harbor seals from an already declining population were estimated to have been killed by the spill. After the spill, oiled seals behaved abnormally, acting lethargic or unwary, and tests showed very high hydrocarbon concentrations in their bile as well as some brain lesions. Of the 182 killer whales that resided in Prince William Sound prior to the spill, 22 were missing afterwards, but it was not known if this unusual disappearance was related to the spill. Other species—fur and ringed seals, Steller sea lions, river otters, bear, mink, and deer—have shown exposure to petroleum hydrocarbons and are the subjects of on-going studies.

No massive die-offs of adult fish resulted from the spill, but several species of coastal and offshore fish (halibut, pollock, cod, and sole) showed evidence of continuing exposure to hydrocarbons. Oil was found, for example, in the gall bladders of pollock in deep offshore areas. Herring studies showed a high percentage of egg mortality and abnormal embryos and larvae in oiled areas in both 1989 and 1990.

After the Exxon Valdez *spill, 144 bald eagles were found dead; several times that number are thought to have been killed and not found.*

Salmon are the primary fish resource of Prince William Sound. No oil has been found in any of the edible flesh of any commercially harvested fish in the area.

JOHN HYDE, ALASKA DEPARTMENT OF FISH AND GAME

The primary fish resource of Prince William Sound—in economic terms—is salmon. In 1989 commercial fishing in oiled areas was closed. Later studies showed that, for wild pink salmon, eggs laid in oiled streams in 1989 suffered a 70% greater mortality than eggs laid in unoiled streams; in 1990, the mortality was 50% greater. Larvae from heavily oiled streams showed gross morphological abnormalities such as club fins and curved spines.

Despite apparent damage to the wild stocks, returns of pink salmon to Prince William Sound in 1990 and 1991 were very high. These were primarily from hatchery stocks that were protected from the spill as fry and eggs, but wild stocks also appeared to have survived well at sea. The return of 1990 (fish that had been outmigrating fry during the spill) was, in fact, a record run; biologists attributed this to higher than usual ocean survival rates due to a rare period of dry, sunny weather that followed the spill and an unusually heavy and long bloom of plankton which provided ample food for the fry. Some scientists have speculated that oil may have helped fuel the plankton bloom, while others have suggested that the large numbers of birds killed by the spill resulted in less-than-usual predation on fry. The return of 1991 (fish hatched from eggs laid a few months after the spill) was unusual in that the main run arrived in Prince William Sound 10 days later than expected—later than they ever had before—and the average size of fish was unusually small.

The assessment studies found no oil in any of the edible flesh of any commercially harvested fish, and the State of Alaska maintained high standards regarding contamination to assure that all harvested fish were safe for human consumption.

Separate assessment data released by the State of Alaska in 1990 indicated that in the intertidal areas of some Prince William Sound salmon streams, biologists were unable to find even a single egg. In addition, samples of herring larvae hatched from eggs collected near oiled shorelines showed 90% with abnormalities compared to 6% with abnormalities in unoiled areas. Since herring hatched from that spawn would not be expected to return as spawners until they were three or four years old, impacts on the commercial fishery were some years away. Another state study found that the enzyme cytochrome P-450E— mentioned earlier as being produced by fish in order to help metabolize hydrocarbons—was present in pink salmon fry and other fish species in oiled areas of Prince William Sound in 1990. This raised concerns about continuing biochemical effects, since the enzyme can convert oil components into carcinogenic and mutagenic compounds. ■

Native Subsistence

The ancestors of these Alutiiq children have lived coastal subsistence lives for thousands of years. Today, villagers typically rely on local foods for up to 85% of their diet.

PRINCE WILLIAM SOUND and other areas of Alaska's southern coast oiled by the *Exxon Valdez* spill are often portrayed as pristine wilderness—home to seabirds, whales, and the occasional silent kayaker. In reality, this part of Alaska includes many small coastal communities, each closely tied to its environment. Residents commonly rely on hunting and fishing for at least part of their food and, in the larger, cash-based communities, livelihoods often come from the sea—through commercial fishing, marine-based tourism, or marine transportation.

Most of the communities have sizable populations of Alaskan Natives, but the 15 smallest, with populations ranging from 47 to 322, are villages primarily of Natives. These people, whose ancestors have lived along this coast for at least 7000 years, have always depended upon the natural resources of the land and, particularly, the sea for their nutritional and cultural needs. Critical to their survival in an often harsh environment has been an acute awareness of the natural world around them, developed from careful observation and shared knowledge.

Although recent years have brought many changes to these people—known as Chugach Aleuts (or Alutiiq) in Prince William Sound and lower Cook Inlet and Koniag Aleuts (or Alutiiq) on Kodiak Island and the Alaska Peninsula—they continue long traditions closely linked to kinship and an intimate relationship with their surroundings. In each community, the people rely on a subsistence-based economy and way of life, with seasonal cash employment and commercial fishing supplementing large harvests of fish, game, and plants. There are no supermarkets in the villages, and food other than what they hunt and gather for themselves is expensive due to transportation costs. Moreover, the hunting, gathering, and preparation activities themselves are an important part of the culture, with much sharing between households and teaching of skills from one generation to the next. It is common to hear references such as "going shopping" applied to taking mussels or seaweed

Clams and cockles are a staple, year-round food for Native people in the area contaminated by the Exxon Valdez *spill. Here, a man digs for butter clams.*

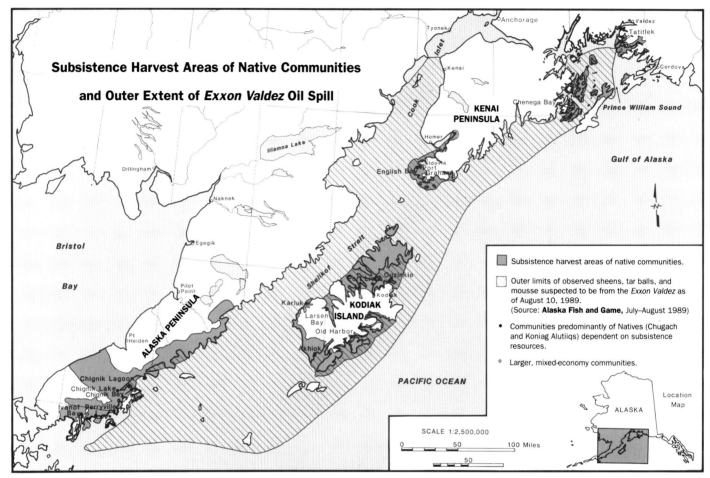

Subsistence Harvest Areas of Native Communities and Outer Extent of *Exxon Valdez* Oil Spill

Legend:

- Subsistence harvest areas of native communities.
- Outer limits of observed sheens, tar balls, and mousse suspected to be from the *Exxon Valdez* as of August 10, 1989. (Source: **Alaska Fish and Game,** July–August 1989)
- Communities predominantly of Natives (Chugach and Koniag Alutiiqs) dependent on subsistence resources.
- Larger, mixed-economy communities.

SCALE 1:2,500,000

0   50   100 Miles

50

ALASKA — Location Map

Source: James A. Fall, "Subsistence Uses of Fish and Wildlife and the *Exxon Valdez* Oil Spill," in *Arctic Issues Digest*, October 1991.

This map shows the subsistence harvest areas of Native communities and the extent to which oil from the Exxon Valdez *spill contaminated water and resources.*

from the beach, or such statements as "When the tide goes out, the table is set."

Prior to the *Exxon Valdez* oil spill, a number of studies had been conducted of subsistence use in various villages. Among the 15 villages that experienced oiling of traditional harvest areas, residents relied on local foods for up to 85% of their diet. On average, subsistence harvests ranged from 200 to 600 pounds per person per year. (This compares to an average purchase, by people in the western United States, of 222 pounds of meat, fish, and poultry per person per year.)

Many different types of foods are harvested—from salmon and halibut to clams, snails, octopus, deer, seals, birds and their eggs, and various wild plants. In study years before the spill, households commonly made use of 20 or more varieties of wild foods, each in its season. Spring was an exciting time of renewal, when people eagerly sought out herring, clams, birds, and young plant shoots. Summer was traditionally the busiest time, when families put away supplies for winter, especially large harvests of salmon; this was also the time when most seasonal, paid work was available. Fall was the time for hunting game and ducks and for berry picking. Winter, a low period of resource harvesting, was when households participated in school activities and Russian Orthodox holiday celebrations and ate food previously preserved; some birds and marine mammals were taken as sources of fresh meat.

Oil came to the "table"

March 24, 1989 was Good Friday and the beginning of spring. The people of Prince William Sound were readying for the arrival of the first schools of herring. Herring—silvery fish something like very large sardines—lay their eggs on kelp and other seaweed. The seaweed and clusters of crunchy, salty eggs are eaten raw, either straight from the sea or dipped in seal oil, with reserves salted away for later in the year. The herring themselves are also caught for both food and bait.

The village closest to the spill was Tatitlek, just six miles from Bligh Reef. Although the winds and current carried the oil away from the village and the immediate area around the village wasn't visibly oiled, people were sickened by the smell of fumes in the first days of the spill. Concerns about oil contamination and the effects of chemical dispersants used on the slick brought all harvesting of marine mammals, fish, and intertidal resources to an immediate halt.

Chenega Bay, on the west side of Prince William Sound, experi-

enced the most direct "hit" of its traditional use areas of all the villages. In an ironic twist of fate, this community suffered its second Good Friday disaster. In 1964, twenty-five years earlier to the day, a tsunami (tidal wave) generated by a major earthquake completely destroyed the old village of Chenega and swept away 23 of its 68 residents. The survivors left the village for other communities in the sound or Anchorage. Only in 1984 was a new village resettled at a site south of the old one—and the people of Chenega reunited with their place and traditions. When spilled oil arrived on their shores, their reacquaintance with their fishing and hunting practices was disrupted, and a strong sense of loss again washed through the community.

As the oil moved out of the sound, along the southeast side of the Kenai Peninsula, to Kodiak Island and the Alaska Peninsula,

©1992 KEN GRAHAM PHOTOGRAPHY

In the Native community of Port Graham, subsistence harvests virtually came to a halt after the Exxon Valdez *spill.*

RON STANECK, ALASKA DEPARTMENT OF FISH AND GAME

A Port Graham woman butchers a seal for its meat and fat. Other foods, such as dried fish, are commonly dipped in seal oil before being eaten.

number of samples from around the spill area but didn't release results until August, five months after the spill and near the end of the summer harvest season. This study concluded that ten "organoleptically clean" samples were found to have no or very low levels of aromatic hydrocarbons—the toxic components of oil—and were safe to eat. Shellfish samples from a heavily oiled area, however, had unacceptably high levels of contamination and were

it continued to foul waters and beaches used for subsistence by Natives and other Alaskans. Natives, so used to paying careful attention to the natural world, observed not only oil, sheens, mousse, and tar balls—but dying birds, dead starfish, barnacles and chitons falling off the rocks they normally adhere to so tenaciously, sick seals, blinded otters, an unnatural quiet, and the smell of death.

What was safe to eat?

Although the oil didn't contaminate all waters and shorelines, its presence in the environment was keenly observed. If fish swam through it, were any of them safe to eat? If deer ate oiled kelp on the beach, where they safe to eat? What were the connections between what people witnessed and what they couldn't see? The spill had created conditions that were utterly different than anything these Natives had ever experienced. With their skills at understanding their surroundings undermined, many lost trust in their own judgments and were afraid to eat traditional foods.

The state government responded to questions about the safety of subsistence foods by recommending the "organoleptic" or taste test. If the item didn't smell or taste of oil, it was considered safe to eat. A pilot study, funded by Exxon, tested a small

deemed unsafe. The villages were notified that finfish could be eaten but that shellfish and molluscs should not be taken from obviously oiled areas.

Villagers were left with many unanswered questions. So few samples were taken, how could they be sure the food they harvested would be safe? How could anyone know that any level of hydrocarbon contamination was safe? Moreover, little or no information was provided on important resources such as deer and seals. People continued to observe unusual animal behaviors and suspect conditions. Some questioned whether a study funded by Exxon could be trusted.

Villagers stopped eating their traditional foods. In the first weeks and months after the spill, most in the oiled areas stopped harvesting wild resources altogether; only later did they begin again with foods they thought they could trust. In the Prince William Sound communities of Tatitlek and Chenega Bay, total subsistence harvests in the year immediately after the spill fell by 57%. In the lower Cook Inlet villages of Port Graham and English Bay, the declines were also sharp—47% and 51%. Villages on Kodiak Island all harvested less after the spill— from 12 to 77% less, depending on the village. Only the villages on the Alaska Peninsula, farthest from the spill, experienced little change.

In addition, fewer kinds of resources were being harvested, as takes shifted from such foods as clams and mussels to greater proportions of other, less suspect foods, such as salmon and halibut. In order to get enough food, some villagers had to travel considerable distances to unpolluted harvest areas or to shop at grocery stores. Others paid expensive air freight charges to ship in groceries.

By far the most common reason for the drop in subsistence harvests was concern about contamination. But there were other reasons. In areas where resources were obviously hard-hit, people didn't feel right about taking what remained. In other cases, residents were employed to clean beaches, and the long hours of work left little time for subsistence activities.

During the 1989 cleanup Exxon sent barges of free food to Tatitlek and Chenega Bay, but the chicken and other processed foods weren't what the people were accustomed to eating. The imported groceries were appreciated but didn't satisfy either their physical appetites or their psychological and spiritual needs for taking, preparing, and sharing wild foods with each other. Native communities from other parts of the state donated subsistence foods of their own, but even this goodwill airlift met only a small portion of the people's requirements. Being given foods—even fresh fish and clean seaweed—was simply not the same as living a life that involves every step of providing what goes on the table.

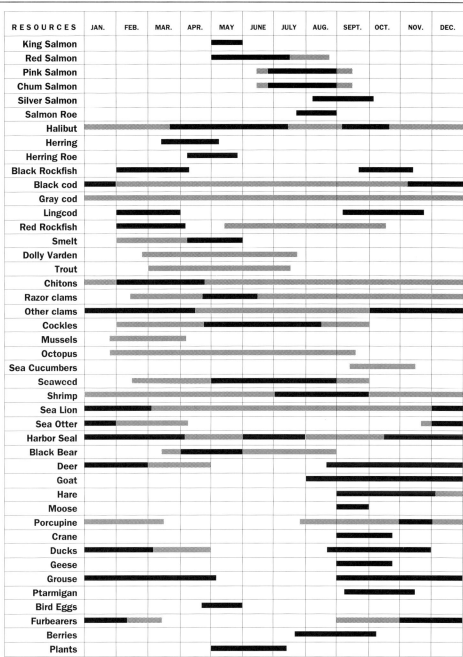

Source: Alaska Department of Fish and Game, Subsistence Department.

Alaska's Native people make use of a wide variety of local foods. This shows the seasonal round of harvest activities in the village of Chenega Bay in 1984–1986. Solid lines indicate the usual harvest season; screened lines mark occasional effort. Foods are typically preserved for use throughout the year and are shared among households.

More than 18 months after the spill, people were still avoiding many subsistence foods. At Chenega Bay, hunters reported finding abnormal livers in seals. Others noticed what seemed to be an unusual number of dead birds and other wildlife.

Further scientific studies confirmed that most foods were safe to eat, since fish and mammals process oil contaminants in their livers and excrete them in bile. Finfish normally don't accumulate hydrocarbons in their edible tissues—except that some studies showed that spawning fish, including salmon, apparently lost some of their metabolizing ability as they neared the time to spawn. Molluscs, however, generally metabolize contaminates at a much slower rate and are therefore much more likely to accumulate hydrocarbons. Mussels from a heavily oiled beach tested at nearly 20,000 parts per billion for aromatic hydrocarbons, compared to mussels from an unoiled control site in southeast Alaska that tested at less than 10 parts per billion.

What is a "safe" level of contamination? Scientists were careful to state that "there are no established guidelines for acceptable levels of aromatic hydrocarbons in foods." In fact, not much is known about the long-term effects of oil on human health, except that aromatic hydrocarbons are considered carcinogenic and mutagenic. Risk to humans comes largely from air pollution, including automobile exhausts and cigarette smoke, but the same hydrocarbons are also present in many commonly-eaten foods—cooked and smoked fish and meats, grains, even fruits and vegetables. In one test of smoked salmon taken from a village in the spill area, a sample of hard-smoked fish (fish hung, typically, over an alder fire for several days to a week) was found to contain more than 20,000 parts per billion of aromatic hydrocarbons.

Residents continued to be suspicious. They questioned whether they should trust the "experts" who were telling them most foods were safe to eat. Weren't these the same people who were saying the oil was "gone" and the beaches "clean"—when they could see with their own eyes that wasn't the case? When contamination was measured in parts per billion, how could they rely on their own skills of observation to tell them what was safe? They were experiencing a loss of control and power that would last as long as they lacked confidence in what they could know for themselves.

Other Natives, despite health warnings and their own misgivings, continued to harvest foods they feared might not be safe. These were the foods they knew, craved, and would continue to eat because they were the foods they had always eaten.

Other effects

The spill and the subsequent cleanup affected the villages in other ways

RON STANECK, ALASKA DEPARTMENT OF FISH AND GAME

A drying rack in English Bay is loaded with split salmon and halibut. Fish dried in this manner will keep for later use.

Alaskan Natives, as they increasingly encounter and adapt to the modern world, still satisfy their nutritional, psychological, and spiritual needs through the harvest of traditional foods.

beyond subsistence. Many Natives—in some villages, every adult who wanted to work—were hired for the first summer of cleaning beaches. The pay of $16.69 per hour resulted in earnings far higher than most had ever earned before. Full-time village jobs—rare and normally coveted—were abandoned. In Port Graham, the positions of alcohol counselor and public safety officer were left empty all summer while everyone scrubbed rocks. For a subsistence-based society that depended very little on the exchange of cash, this influx of money resulted in significant changes in their lives—everything from being able to buy new skiffs and home satellite dishes to running into trouble with the I.R.S. at tax time.

Psychological stress from having their lives so utterly disrupted was also apparent in village life. With parents away working on cleanup jobs, some children experienced a sense of insecurity. Elders found there was less room for them to engage in their traditional roles as teachers and advisors. In some communities, competition for jobs and a new disparity between haves and have-nots resulted in resentment—not just against Exxon

and its contractors but among villagers themselves; traditions of sharing and goodwill suffered. Feelings of helplessness, fear, and anger resulted in an increase in family problems and drinking following the spill.

The villagers experienced, as well, increased contact with outsiders and layers of government with whom they formerly had little association. Some villages were virtually inundated with other cleanup workers looking for jobs, members of the media, and oil industry representatives. Villagers learned, crash-course style, how to make their concerns known, who to talk to, and what kinds of stories the press was interested in reporting.

This abrupt introduction to a world of regular paychecks, frequent travel, competition, and outsiders with new and different ideas may, in the long run, alter village life more than the oil spill itself. Change has been coming to Alaska for a long time and has gradually been influencing Native villagers in their transition from traditional ways to an accommodation with the modern world. The wreck of the *Exxon Valdez* surely accelerated the process for those in the path of the spilled oil. ■

Cleanup

Exxon mounted the largest shoreline cleanup operation ever undertaken. Technologies ranged from wiping rocks by hand and scraping with trowels to applying high-pressure hot-water washes, chemicals, and oil-eating microorganisms.

In 1989 11,000 cleanup workers were hired. The presence of so many people on previously isolated beaches had an environmental impact of its own.

A VARIETY OF TECHNOLOGIES designed to contain, recover, and clean up spilled oil exist, but none are adequate for dealing with major spills in offshore, remote, or sensitive areas. The *Exxon Valdez* disaster proved the inadequacy of available cleanup equipment and methods—most of which have changed little in the last two decades—and catalyzed their reevaluation.

Technologies range from removing oil from the surface of water with simple buckets or mechanical skimmers to shoreline cleaning with shovels and trowels, cold and hot water washes, or oil-eating microorganisms. Each has advantages and disadvantages, and in the case of a large spill combinations of many technologies would likely be employed. In some cases, an active cleanup program can do more harm than good, and the best remedy may be to do nothing—to allow the natural biological and physical processes to function without additional injury.

Even in the best of circumstances, only a portion of spilled oil can ever be recovered. Historically, no more than 10 to 20% of oil has been recovered from large spills; estimates for the *Exxon Valdez*, after a cleanup expenditure of over two billion dollars, run between 3 and 24%, with the State of Alaska's best guess at 8%. Experts consider it unlikely that technical advances will ever result in recovery of more than 50% of the oil from a major spill.

Recovery of oil from water

Methods of recovering oil from open water include the use of a wide variety of absorbents, containment booms and skimmers, pumps, and dredges.

Oil can be absorbed by a variety of materials and then removed from the material, such as by being squeezed through rollers, or disposed of with the material. The simplest types of absorbers are natural materials such as straw and dried sugar cane stocks. Straw, which traps oil in its fibers, can collect oil weighing between 8 and 30 times its own weight. Synthetic materials

Booms are used like floating fences to try to corral oil so that it can be picked up or to prevent it from entering sensitive areas.

Skimmers are often used in conjunction with booms, to pick up surface oil once it's been corraled. There are at least 14 different kinds of skimmers among the categories of weir, suction, boom, vortex, and moving surface. They commonly employ some sort of pumping or suction device and a mechanism for separating oil from water. Skimmers can work well in calm water on small spills, such as when a small amount of oil leaks in a harbor during a loading operation. They do not, however, work well in heavy seas or on large spills in the open ocean. They have a relatively low recovery rate and tend to clog with debris or weathered oil and break down. They also require the availability of additional storage capacity so that recovered oil can be offloaded.

A number of products exist that can alter the consistency of oil so that it's more readily picked up from the water. Gelling agents, for example, change liquid oil into gelatinous masses. One type uses a chemical powder to "rubberize" the oil. As a result, the oil adheres better to equipment surfaces, making it easier for certain skimmers to pick it up. Another type causes oil to coagulate so that it won't emulsify or mix with water. Many of these products are still in experimental phases. Generally, they must be used soon after the oil spills, before it weathers.

can be produced that are both water repellent and very good oil absorbers, and these can be reused. Absorbents, however, are not very practical in dealing with large at-sea spills.

Booms are long, floating, tubular barriers fitted with underwater "skirts"; they sometimes also have splash shields attached to the top of them. They operate as floating fences to surround, contain, and deflect spreading oil slicks. Homemade booms can be made from logs lashed together, with weighted plywood skirts. Some booms are made of absorbent material designed to soak up oil. Others are made of fireproof material so that the oil within them can be burned. Booms, depending on their design and suitability for conditions, can be effective in containing oil slicks in calm to moderate seas. They, however, take considerable time and labor to deploy and maintain. Rough seas or fast currents can cause oil to wash over or slip under them.

These salmon hatchery pens in Prince William Sound were guarded by a final double barrier of deflection boom.

Treating oil on water

Aside from mechanical recovery, surface oil can be treated in a number of ways that do not involve its physical removal from the water. These include dispersal with chemicals, burning, sinking, and bioremediation.

Chemical dispersants sprayed onto an oil slick are intended to break the oil into small droplets that can spread into the water column or sink into bottom sediments. Dispersants are essentially detergents. The advantage of their use is that, under some circumstances, they can help clear oil from the surface and prevent it from washing ashore. However, the oil remains in the water or sediments, from which it can enter the food web. In addition, some dispersants are toxic to marine life—even more than oil. The scientific community remains divided over their use.

Test results indicate that dispersants are not particularly effective. They must be applied very early in a spill since oil becomes less dispersable as its light ends evaporate, and they must be agitated by rough seas to activate properly. Dispersants must be delivered by aircraft or vessels that are especially equipped with spray systems. Large quantities are needed—on the order of one gallon of dispersant for every 20 gallons of oil.

Oil slicks can sometimes be burned, but only if they are of sufficient thickness and have adequate volatility—which means burning, to work, must take place very quickly after a spill, usually in the first day. Fire is set using floating ignitors, incendiary bombs, or napalm. Up to 90% of freshly-spilled oil can be eliminated in this way. However, even under optimal conditions, burning leaves a tarry residue

Slicks of fresh oil can sometimes be burned, although burning produces toxic smoke and leaves a tarry residue.

and produces toxic smoke.

Sinking agents such as powdered chalk have also been used to remove surface oil. The idea is to have the oil stick to fine particles so that the combined density causes the oil to sink. Sinking agents have, however, proven difficult to apply, and results have been poor. In one test of several agents, none was found to be effective; after first sinking, the oil slowly returned to the surface. Other experiments and use found that when the agents did carry the oil to the seabed, both the powder and oil exposed marine life to their toxic properties and fouled fishing nets and catch.

Bioremediation is the use of microbes to break down oil. Certain types of marine bacteria known to consume oil—petrophiles—can be introduced, or naturally occurring ones can be increased by the use of fertilizers. In theory, these will metabolize at least parts of the oil into mineral components, and more of them will do it faster. Although fertilizers have often been used to stimulate biodegradation of oil spills on land, only rarely have such treatments been monitored for effectiveness in marine systems. Bioremediation on water is of questionable value. Nutrients added directly to the sea are rapidly diluted, and, because the process takes time to work, are unlikely to have any effect before oil goes ashore. In addition, fertilizers can dramatically increase plant growth and might reduce oxygen in the water needed by fish and shellfish. (Bioremediation on shorelines is discussed in the following section.)

Shoreline cleanup

Oiled shorelines can be cleaned using a variety of technologies. The particular strategies used will depend on the type of shoreline—rocky cliffs versus sandy beach, for example. In some situations no human intervention may be most appropriate, leaving the natural processes to work.

Oil can be, and is, cleaned from beaches and shorelines with the most unsophisticated methods—shovels and rakes, garden trowels, and various absorbent materials. Rocks can be wiped or washed off, cliffs can be scraped, tar balls and chunks of asphalt can be picked up by hand. Oily sediments can be shoveled into buckets and hauled to disposal sites. Equipment such as bulldozers and backhoes can be used to move rocks and excavate sediments.

Shoreline treatment with chemicals—similar to the dispersants sometimes used at sea—can cause oil to loosen from rock so that it can be removed. Such treatment is controversial because of direct contact with intertidal organisms, some of which have little or no mobility. Some cleaning chemicals are toxic, and all result in spreading the oil over a larger area, which can impact more organisms. Moreover, studies suggest that such chemicals are generally ineffective on stranded oil. In an area where spill damage is primarily economic rather than ecological, such as an industrial harbor, some chemicals might be used to advantage.

Cold water washes involve pumping sea water through fire hoses onto oiled beaches at low tide to dislodge oil. As the tide comes in over the beaches, skimming vessels can pick up the oily surface water. This technique, which is relatively harmless to the environment, works quite well on fresh oil. It is not very effective with weathered oil, and too much pressure can drive oil deeper into the sediments. Agitating a beach with shovels or

©1992 KEN GRAHAM PHOTOGRAPHY

Here, oil is washed off a beach so that it can be picked up from the water's surface by a skimmer.

rakes during a wash leads to releasing more oil than merely letting the water soak the beach.

Hot water high pressure washes are used to blast weathered oil from rocks and cliffs. Hot water can also be pumped into the shoreline to dislodge trapped oil. Detergents and solvents are sometimes added to break up the oil. While hot water dislodges oil better than cold water and can be very efficient in removing oil, steam and chemicals act to sterilize beaches, killing all life on them. High pressure can also drive oil deeper into the sediments.

Bioremediation (also discussed, above, as an at-sea technology) generally relies on the use of nitrogen-rich fertilizers to stimulate the growth of naturally occurring microbes that "eat" oil. The fertilizer is spread on beaches, either in liquid form or as pellets designed for time release. In theory, microbes first attack the fertilizer and increase their numbers, then turn to oil for nourishment. Fertilizers, which contain chemicals, can be hazardous to birds and wildlife, especially when first applied.

Bioremediation is still very much a new technology, and long-term effects of the fertilizers are unknown. Because so many other factors are at work on a recovering shoreline and because natural biodegradation is imperfectly understood, it is very difficult to determine whether, or how much, bioremediation assists the natural process. In the short-run, some studies have found that bioremediation actually slows hydrocarbon degradation; the microbes prefer to eat the fertilizer instead of the oil. In the longer-term, some scientists believe that—at least in places deficient in nutrients— bioremediation can increase rates of biodegradation two- or three-fold. Other scientists, however, say meaningful data has yet to support such a claim. Results take time and should not be confused with immediate visible changes; the chemical carrier agents in some fertilizers act as a detergent to loosen oil and wash it into the substrate or out with the tide.

The most basic of all cleanup processes belongs to nature and time. Natural degradation takes place not only as microbes and other organisms metabolize oil and its components but as wind, rain, waves, and snow dislodge oil from beaches and disperse oil particles. It is a slow process, especially in areas sheltered from the elements. Nevertheless, many scientists believe, based on case histories, that in most shoreline habitats most cleanup technologies increase immediate ecological damage and delay recovery, and that natural degradation is to be preferred. Cleanup decisions are often made based not on scientific criteria but for reasons of aesthetics, economics, or political and public pressure.

Disposal of materials from cleanup operations

Following an oil spill a major environmental problem is how to dispose of wastes generated by the cleanup. These include oil itself (which might be whipped into an emulsion that's largely water), oil-coated seaweeds, dead birds and animals, and contaminated sand and beach materials. Wastes also include supplies used in the cleanup such as chemicals, oily gloves, and all kinds of absorbent materials used to contain and soak up oil.

The ideal situation is to transport recovered oil to a refinery for reprocessing. When the oil is mixed with other materials or is in such a state or concentration that it's not economically extractable, wastes must be either incinerated or buried in specially-constructed landfills where the oil will not be allowed to contaminate groundwater. All of these disposal methods involve additional environmental impacts; transportation involves burning fuel, incineration puts hydrocarbons into the air, and burial adds to landfill problems.

The *Exxon Valdez* cleanup

Immediately after the spill, Exxon's public affairs manager promised that Exxon would "pick up, one way or another, all the oil that's out there." With time, everyone involved acknowledged that all of the oil would not—could not—be cleaned up. The talk changed from "clean" to "environmentally stabilized," and eventually beaches were simply described as "treated."

Under United States law, primary cleanup responsibility after a spill lies with the spiller. The federal government takes over only if a spiller's response is inadequate. In the case of the *Exxon Valdez*, the initial response was made by Alyeska, the

Water washing with too much pressure can drive oil deeper into the sediments. Hot water dislodges oil better than cold water but is deadly to beach organisms.

consortium of oil companies which had an approved spill contingency plan for Prince William Sound. Exxon, the owner of the tanker, took over before the first day was out, leading to confusion about who was in charge. Throughout the cleanup process, Exxon initiated the various cleanup operations, while federal and state agencies used their oversight responsibilities to try to influence and direct the activities.

A wide range of cleanup technologies was used by Exxon, Alyeska, local governments, and volunteers. No one was prepared for a spill of such size, and there was little success in containing and recovering oil before it hit beaches. Fourteen hours passed before an equipment barge carrying skimmers and boom even reached the tanker, but this amount of equipment couldn't begin to address the problem. Additional skimmers and boom materials were flown in from around the world, but it was too little too late. During the first 72 hours after the spill, very little oil was picked up—only 126,000 gallons, or 1% of the volume. Moreover, there were few vessels available to hold what oil the skimmers did pick up. Full skimmers sat idle, waiting to be emptied.

NANCY MENNING

Bioremediation is an experimental technique of applying fertilizers to stimulate the growth of naturally occurring microbes that "eat" oil. In the photograph, the light areas are treated beach, the dark areas untreated. Such dramatic visual changes are not due to an increase in microbial activity in treated areas but to the fertilizer's chemical carrier agents, which act as a detergent to loosen oil from rocks.

Mechanical skimmers were outperformed by a simple bucket brigade organized by fishermen. A single fishing boat, on its best day, recovered 2500 gallons using five-gallon buckets, while Exxon's best skimmer recovered just 1200 gallons per day. The most successful use of boom was also by fishermen who, under state guidance, deployed it around salmon hatcheries.

After three days the oil became so viscous that it was much more difficult to pick up with skimmers—and it was pushed ashore by a storm.

Exxon pressed to use dispersants early on, but these were not widely used for a variety of reasons. Contingency plans referred to the need for dispersants in some spills, but did not discuss under what conditions they should be used. The state and federal governments were concerned about their use, particularly with major fish runs about to enter the sound. In any case, there was only a small amount of the chemicals available—perhaps enough to disperse 8% of the spill—and no aircraft or application equipment suitable to spray or dump it. In the end, dispersants were used only in some limited tests before the oil was too spread out and weathered to be successfully treated.

One effort to burn the oil was attempted on the second day of the spill. Oil was collected behind fireproof booms and ignited. Approximately 15,000 gallons was consumed, but heavy black smoke drifted over the community of Tatitlik. By the time more burning was planned and approved, the oil was too spread out and weathered.

Once the oil impacted the coast, the cleanup effort shifted to the 1244 miles of oiled shoreline. In 1989 11,000 workers were hired to wipe rocks, shovel oily sediments, pick up tar balls, and treat beaches with cold and hot water washes. Booms and skimmers were used offshore to recover oil washed from beaches. The entire cleanup was plagued by problems of logistics and disagreements over treatment methods, jurisdiction of various agencies, and operation completion criteria.

Tests were conducted on several sections of heavily oiled coastline with the chemical Corexit, a kerosene-based substance newly developed by Exxon's research branch. Although Exxon believed Corexit should be widely applied to beaches to loosen oil, the state was concerned about use of a new, untested, and potentially toxic chemical. The state concluded that, although the chemical could release the oil's bond to the substrate, it could not enhance collection. The amount of oil retrieved from the chemical test areas never surpassed the control sites of regular water washing. In fact, when the volume of chemical applied was factored in, there was a negative return. That is, at one site where 73 gallons of Corexit were sprayed, only 10 gallons of both oil and Corexit were recovered during the ensuing wash and skimming.

Bioremediation was another of Exxon's favored treatment choices. Oiled beaches were treated with two kinds of fertilizers—a liquid one called Inipol and a granular one called Customblen. Both are nitrogen-phosphorus fertilizers designed to enhance biodegradation of the oil by microorganisms already present in the environment. (These microorganisms, which evolved to eat the terpenes—plant hydrocarbons—produced by the native spruce trees, are able to metabolize some chemically-similar hydrocarbons found in North Slope crude.) Chemicals in the fertilizers are considered a risk to wildlife, and cleanup crews used noisemakers and balloons in an attempt to keep birds and other animals off newly treated beaches.

The short-term results of applying the fertilizers were inconclusive, although treated beaches appeared cleaner due to chemical solvents included in Inipol. A year later, a study to try to determine the effectiveness of bioremediation found that the populations of hydrocarbon-degrading microbes were higher on treated plots than on untreated plots. This suggests that biodegradation of hydrocarbons was enhanced by the addition of fertilizers. However, given the complexity of the environment and the fact that Prince William Sound is already a nutrient-rich area, the study could not directly prove that oil contamination was being reduced due to enhanced microbial activity. More monitoring will be necessary before any conclusions can be reached about bioremediation's long-term results in Prince William Sound.

Another bioremediation test involved inoculation, or the releasing of foreign, oil-degrading microorganisms to beaches in the sound. This test, like others in Texas, produced no demonstrated benefit. Scientists believe that naturally occurring populations of microbes are generally sufficient and better adapted to metabolizing oil than introduced varieties.

In addition to Exxon's cleaning, some local governments and volunteers organized their own cleanups. These usually relied on low-tech methods of picking up oil with hand tools. One volunteer effort used an innovative homemade rock washing machine.

In the summers of 1990 and 1991 Exxon's scaled-down cleanup operations continued. Some oiled storm berms were relocated with backhoes and bulldozers to lower sections of beach where oil could be floated off by the tide and picked up. Some tilling was done to free oil from sediments. Tar mats were broken up and collected. Fertilizers were repeatedly applied. Little additional cleanup was expected after 1991.

Longer-term study will be necessary to determine the success of Exxon's cleanup. Beach cleaning itself altered the shape and structure of beaches and affected intertidal organisms. In some cases, treated areas were stripped of flora and fauna and showed little recolonization a year later, compared to oiled beaches that received little or no treatment. Fine sand and gravel flushed from upper elevations to lower ones often buried and killed organisms that had survived the spill. Such areas may take longer to recover than less disturbed areas.

The Exxon cleanup generated enormous amounts of waste. Some of the absorbent materials were incinerated in Alaska, but the vast majority of oily debris was shipped to a hazardous waste landfill in Oregon—in 1989, some 31,000 tons. Much of this was oiled sediments—sand and gravel—that was removed rather than being cleaned and returned. A small amount of recovered oil was refined into a fuel used for drying cement.

More fuel—18 million gallons of refined products, mostly gasoline and diesel—was consumed by cleanup equipment than was originally spilled. Six million gallons were used just to operate the heaters for the hot-water beach washes. Additional oil was consumed in manufacturing and shipping the cleanup supplies and equipment and in transporting workers to and around Alaska. All of this oil inevitably posed additional risk as it was transported from drilling site to refinery to the site of its ultimate use, and the process of burning it added additional hydrocarbons to what was previously a relatively pristine environment. ■

The Exxon cleanup resulted in mountains of waste that needed to be disposed of by incinerating or burying in hazardous waste landfills.

Animal Rescue and Rehabilitation

©1992 ALISSA CRANDALL

Until the Exxon Valdez *spill, there had been little experience anywhere in the world with capturing and treating oiled mammals. More than 430 people participated in Exxon's sea otter rehabilitation effort, 344 otters were handled, and 197 were eventually released to the wild. The costs to Exxon were high—$80,000 per otter "saved."*

The stress of capture, transport, treatment, and captivity can contribute to the mortality of animals already weakened by contact with oil. Rescue workers had to force-feed many animals too weakened to feed themselves.

WHENEVER THERE'S A MAJOR OIL SPILL at sea, birds and wildlife that feed or rest on the ocean's surface risk heavy contamination. People react by wanting to rescue, clean, and care for these victims. Scientists generally believe that such rescues, except in the case of endangered species or populations, have no ecological significance.

Historically, rescue efforts have largely failed, with mortality of rescued birds exceeding 80%. However, after years of experience and with increased understanding about oil's toxic effects, bird mortality rates have been reduced to as little as 15%. There is less experience with mammals, although the *Exxon Valdez* spill provided a tremendous amount of experience in treating sea otters.

The cleaning and rehabilitation process

Oiled birds and mammals typically arrive at cleaning centers with a host of medical problems—hypothermia, dehydration, shock, stress, and anemia. They may suffer both from the oil's effects on their feathers or fur, which causes them to lose water repellency and insulating qualities, and from the problems of ingesting oil through feeding and preening or grooming. Where they have breathed fumes, they also have probably suffered lung damage. Once in captivity, they commonly develop additional problems—more stress and stress-related injuries and disease, eye disease, malnutrition, and foot and leg problems.

The first step in treating birds is to stabilize them by keeping them warm and quiet and by feeding them. Force-feeding of formula is usually necessary. Cleaning takes place only after the birds are stabilized and involves repeated washings with a detergent. The dishwashing detergent Dawn has been found to be most suitable. This washing and rinsing process can take an hour or more for each bird. The birds are then thoroughly dried. After cleaning, birds must bathe and preen in order to recover the natural oils that make their feathers water-repellent;

Of the 1589 birds brought to cleaning centers following the Exxon Valdez *spill, half died and half were released after treatment.*

normal grooming. This might be accelerated with the application of squalene (a fish oil used in manufacturing pharmaceuticals) to replace the natural oils removed by washing, but such use is still being tested and evaluated. Cleaned otters are held in pre-release facilities where they can swim, groom, and eat well until they regain their strength.

Any time birds or mammals are brought together for treatment, disease is always a threat. Weakened animals are more vulnerable, and epidemics can spread quickly through a rehabilitation center. Diseases might also be carried back to healthy populations when animals are released. Additionally, there is always the danger that contact with domestic pets might infect otters or seals with distemper or parvovirus—and then be transferred to wild populations.

The *Exxon Valdez* spill

The wildlife rehabilitation effort following the *Exxon Valdez* spill was the largest, most expensive, and most controversial ever attempted. It demonstrated that many issues of animal rescue and rehabilitation following a spill are yet to be resolved.

As with the cleanup operation, responsibility for animal rescue and rehabilitation fell to Exxon, with government agencies assuming monitoring roles. Divisions of authority caused continual problems in mounting an effective program. At first, the capture effort lagged far behind the need; when it began in earnest many birds and otters were already dead and the treatment facilities were quickly overtaxed.

Exxon contracted with the International Bird Rescue Center, headquartered in Berkeley, California, which set up bird cleaning operations in Valdez, Seward, Homer, Kodiak, and Anchorage. A scientist from the Hubbs Marine Research Center at Sea World was hired to operate a sea otter center in Valdez; other facilities followed in Seward, Homer, and Kodiak. Hundreds of people, most of them volunteers, were involved in the efforts.

More than 430 people participated just in the sea otter program, including biologists and veterinarians who came from all over the country. Very high mortalities occurred among the first

this normally takes two or three days. Birds can be released when they are strong and healthy and have a completely water-repellent plumage.

The system for treating sea otters is very similar. They are first medically stabilized and sedated. In some cases, activated carbon is pumped into stomachs to absorb toxic hydrocarbons. After repeated washings with a solution of Dawn detergent, they are thoroughly rinsed and dried. Full restoration of the fur's water repellency and insulation takes 5–10 days with

otters rescued. Autopsies showed the animals to have severely damaged internal organs and deficient immune systems. The stress of capture and handling was thought to have contributed to the deaths, but the toxic effects of inhaling and ingesting oil were the primary causes. Of the 344 otters handled in all, 110 died, 197 were eventually released to the wild, and 37 were sent to aquariums. The cost to Exxon was about $80,000 per animal "saved."

There is considerable evidence that the apparently-rehabilitated sea otters did not survive well in the long-run. After being treated at rehabilitation facilities and then held in outdoor pens until they appeared fully recovered, 45 otters were implanted with radio transmitters and released into an unoiled area of Prince William Sound. After 20 days, all were alive and vigorous. However, after eight months, 28 were either dead (13) or missing and presumed dead (15). The greatest mortality within that time period occurred with the onset of winter, and otters continued to die, at a lesser rate, after the eight months. These rates of dead and missing are much higher than those normally observed for adult sea otters in the area. For example, of 58 otters similarly implanted with transmitters in 1987, all were alive after eight months of monitoring.

Aside from sea otters, few other mammals were rescued and rehabilitated. Some harbor seals were brought in for cleaning or because they were orphaned, but large-scale rescue was not practical for large animals, and no other species were as immediately susceptible as otters to the ill effects of oiling.

The extent of the spill and the remoteness of much of the marine bird habitat made it difficult to find and rescue birds. Moreover, government agencies were reluctant to get involved in a bird rescue operation, and Exxon moved slowly to assume the responsibility. The number of birds brought to treatment centers—1589—is tiny compared to the roughly half-million thought to have died from oiling. In contrast, after a 1971 spill in San Francisco Bay that killed 20,000 birds, approximately 2000 oiled individuals were captured and cleaned.

Of the loons, grebes, cormorants, seaducks, murres, and other birds received at the cleaning centers, half died and half were

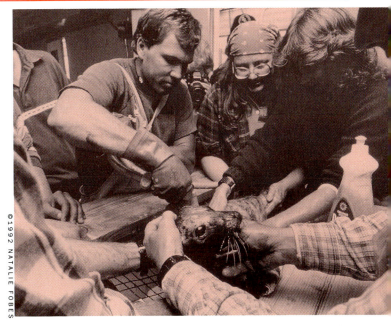

© 1992 NATALIE FOBES

It takes many hands to clean each animal. Here, a seal goes through the lengthy washing process.

released after treatment. The expense for each rehabilitated bird was about $30,000. A small number of eagles, ill from eating oiled carrion, were captured and rehabilitated in separate raptor facilities at a cost of $42,000 each. There was no follow-up monitoring regarding the long-term survival of rehabilitated birds.

Although there were apparently no very serious transmissions of disease as a result of the rescue and rehabilitation programs, contagious diseases were always a concern. At one point the Alaska Department of Fish and Game recommended that no otters be released to the wild because of the possibility they might have been infected with canine diseases. (Captured otters were transported in used dog kennels—the kind designed for airplane travel.) At another point there was an outbreak of herpes-like mouth lesions among otters at the Seward facility; the lesions were thought not to be a major concern after similar ones were found in wild populations. Among birds, an outbreak of aspergillosis (a highly contagious fungal disease) occurred at the Valdez facility.

The next spill?

Numerous recommendations for improved animal rescue and rehabilitation resulted from the *Exxon Valdez* experience. Perhaps the most important is that government agencies, not the spiller, should have responsibility for wildlife rehabilitation programs following major spills. Responses must be planned ahead of time and be assured of adequate resources, including funding and trained personnel.

Some scientists have suggested that otters rescued from oil spills and later released should, in the future, not be called "rehabilitated" but only "treated," to reflect the conclusions that such animals are not returned to a normal state. Although much was learned from the *Exxon Valdez* experience, they question whether such capture and treatment programs should be repeated.

Above: *Once all the oil is washed from their fur, otters are kept in special holding pens until their grooming restores natural oils and they've recovered sufficient strength to be returned to the wild.*

Left: *A cleaned duck, insignificant to total populations, is released. The fundamental issue still at stake is what degree of human intervention after an oil spill benefits individual animals, populations, or species.*

One question that has yet to be resolved concerns whether lightly-oiled animals, particularly otters, are better off being captured and cleaned (and subjected to the risks associated with capture, transport, treatment, and holding) or left alone in the wild. Although some tests and controlled experiments were proposed during the course of the *Exxon Valdez* rescue to address this question, none was successfully completed.

The fundamental issue still at stake is what degree of human intervention benefits the animals, both as individuals and as species or populations. On the one hand, rehabilitation efforts are extremely costly and normally save an insignificant number of animals in a population while often extending the pain and suffering of those captured. On the other hand, who can disre-

gard innocent victims that might be saved? In any spill or other disaster, people react to suffering with heart-felt emotion and humane instincts.

One argument for continuing expensive and questionable rehabilitation efforts is that a future spill might place an entire population at risk. There are enough otters in Prince William Sound and the Gulf of Alaska that populations are expected to recover—with or without the rehabilitation effort—but what if the next spill happens in the range of the threatened California sea otter? The learning that took place during the *Exxon Valdez* response may lead to better understandings and treatment improvements more critically needed in the future. ■

Recovery and Restoration

PATRICK ENDRES

Scientists dig test pits to measure the depth to which oil can be found in beach sediments and to study the oil's movement, toxicity, rate of degradation, and effect on the ecosystem.

ECOLOGICAL RECOVERY is defined as the reestablishment of a healthy biological community in which plants and animals characteristic of the original community are present and functioning normally. The community may not have the identical composition or age structure as that which was present before the damage. Since any ecosystem is constantly changing, it is unlikely that one that has recovered from an oil spill will be the same as it was before the spill, and it is difficult to determine how different the recovered ecosystem is from the one that would have evolved naturally without a spill.

In general, organisms begin to recolonize an area as soon as they are able to tolerate the conditions, so that the recovery process begins fairly quickly. Recovery depends on a variety of factors including the kind and quantity of oil spilled, the habitat involved, temperatures, time of year, whether toxic dispersants are used, what methods of cleanup (if any) are employed, and the amount of recontamination that occurs. Recovery is fastest in open water. Rocky intertidal areas which are exposed to turbulent (high-energy) conditions also recover relatively quickly. Soft intertidal and subtidal sediments take the longest time to recover.

Recovery rates, because of a lack of long-term study as well as the factors mentioned above, are difficult to predict; in some cases the time scale is not yet known. Temperate areas are generally associated with possible recovery times of 10–20 years. While the recolonization by some species can be quite rapid, imbalances can persist for decades. As much as 30 years (3–6 generations) may be required for the recovery of a normal age distribution of clams. Some species don't even begin to decline until a year or more after a spill.

Polar waters take longer than temperate waters to recover, both because cold temperatures retard evaporation and microbial activity and because species in cold environments tend to be

A high energy shoreline exposed to pounding seas will recover more rapidly than areas such as mud flats and marshes.

slow-growing, highly seasonal, and slow to reach reproductive age. Any interference with the short period of summer production can prevent successful feeding, breeding, and the building of reserves needed for winter survival.

Typically, some level of recovery will begin while oil-spill effects, including delayed mortality, are still taking place. For example, one year after the *Exxon Valdez* spill, one study beach had begun to be recolonized by tiny new barnacles (called barnacle sets) and a new growth of intertidal *Fucus* (rockweed) plants. At the same time on the same beach, blue mussels were in the last stages of loosing their fibrous attachments to rock; this effect of the oil caused them to drop off and eventually be killed by predators, rough seas, or other elements of an unprotected environment.

Restoration

Restoration is a human intervention process that follows a spill, any cleanup that might be attempted, and an assessment of the damages. Its goal is to hasten recovery. In some cases, however, decisions will be made that it is most appropriate to allow natural recovery to take place without further intervention.

Restoration ecology is an emerging field that still lacks much basic information needed to make restoration efforts efficient and expeditious. Because every ecosystem, especially in the marine environment, is unique, any restoration program must itself be uniquely designed. Programs normally focus on both restoration of habitat and restoration of organisms.

Federal regulations specifically define restoration: "'Restoration' or 'rehabilitation' means actions undertaken to return an injured resource to its baseline condition, as measured in terms of the injured resource's physical, chemical, or biological properties or the services it previously provided."

Restoration activities, again specified by federal regulations, fall into three categories: direct restoration, replacement, and acquisition of equivalent resources. Direct restoration would be implemented on-site, within some or all of a damaged ecosystem, while replacement and acquisition projects might take place in another area altogether. An example of direct restora-

tion would be transplanting plants and animals from a healthy environment to an area (when it is no longer toxic) where populations of the same species of plants and animals were reduced or eliminated. An example of replacement would be the substitution of a new resource for an injured resource, such as using a fish hatchery to create a new fishery stock to make up for a devastated natural run. Acquisition of equivalent resources could include the purchase of undamaged and unprotected wildlife habitats as an alternative to direct restoration of injured habitats.

Before any restoration program can be developed, there must be adequate information on damages, especially long-term, to the ecosystem. Even then, the outcome of a course of action in restoration cannot be absolutely predicted.

The Restoration Process for Alaska

Soon after the *Exxon Valdez* spill, both President Bush and Alaska Governor Cowper expressed their desires that the environment of Prince William Sound and the Gulf of Alaska be restored. Federal and state agencies initiated 72 scientific studies designed to determine damages, both in terms of specific resource injuries and their corresponding monetary values.

In late 1989 an interagency Restoration Planning Work Group was established to develop and coordinate restoration activities. The goal of this restoration planning effort was to identify appropriate measures that could be taken to restore the ecological health and uses of natural resources affected by the spill. Once potential activities were identified, they would be evaluated in terms of technical feasibility, environmental benefit, and cost. Public participation was to be an integral part of the process.

A limited number of small-scale studies were conducted in 1990 and 1991 to evaluate the feasibility of various restoration techniques. One such study related to the reestablishment of *Fucus*, a plant that was extensively damaged by both the spill and the cleanup efforts. Another identified upland habitats used by wildlife, including marbled murrelets and harlequin ducks, affected by the spill. Additional studies were designed to

Restoration funds may be spent to purchase and protect privately held lands such as these small but important seabird nesting islands.

monitor natural recoveries, identify salmon and herring stocks, select sites for stabilization with beach rye, and investigate the use of artificial reefs for fish and shellfish.

Clearly, the possible options for restoration following the *Exxon Valdez* spill are limitless. Results of the damage assessment studies and the amount of available money, as well as public opinion, will help determine the specific strategies. Scoping meetings held in Alaska in 1990 produced long lists of suggestions from the public, even though results of the damage assessment studies had not been released. Most people supported an active restoration program that would approach the damaged ecosystem as a whole and try to restore its overall integrity. Many stressed the need for continuing study and suggested that an environmental trust fund could assure funding for long-term monitoring and research.

Many specific ideas mentioned at the scoping meetings involved the rehabilitation of habitat and efforts to speed recolonization. For example, suggestions were made to reestablish beach grasses in areas damaged by oil and cleanup activities. Ideas for helping fish populations included constructing spawning channels, increasing food supplies through lake fertilization, and raising and releasing fish from hatcheries. Another suggestion to improve the nesting habitat of damaged seabirds was to eliminate foxes that were introduced to certain islands in the past as part of the fur trade.

Most speakers agreed that further disturbance from human activities should be minimized, and some suggested using restoration funds to increase enforcement of existing laws regarding hunting, fishing, and the maintenance of buffer strips along streams.

Nearly all participants agreed that recovery could be speeded through land protection, such as direct purchase of important habitat. Since much of the affected area is Native corporation land slated for logging, some suggested purchase of portions of these lands to maintain water quality and protect breeding habitats. Others proposed the purchase of important and equivalent habitats outside of the damaged areas or the purchase of timber rights, oil lease options, or conservation easements. New wilderness and refuge areas, cooperative land management agreements, and habitat conservation tax credits were also suggested.

Other participants viewed the spill and restoration program as an opportunity to raise public awareness about the need for oil spill prevention and changes in energy policies and laws. Some proposed that restoration funds be spent on environmental education designed to encourage better protection of the resources damaged by the spill.

Exxon settlement

A court settlement between the state and federal governments and Exxon in October 1991 provides for Exxon to pay one billion dollars, over ten years, into a restoration fund. Under the terms of the settlement, money from the fund must be spent on restoration and enhancement of resources and services.

"Enhancement" expands the scope of what might be done in the region beyond the previous understanding regarding restoration. Enhancement activities might include, for example, adding hatchery fish beyond what would compensate for spill losses. It might also, according to some proposals, involve activities such as building roads and recreational facilities, to "enhance" opportunities for more people to access and enjoy Prince William Sound.

The restoration fund will be overseen by six trustees—three each from the state and federal governments—who must agree unanimously on any expenditures from the fund. ■

Will It Happen Again?

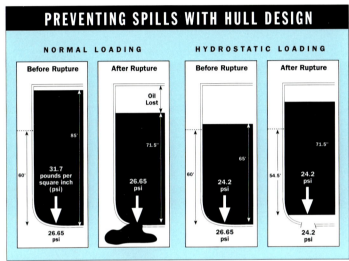

PREVENTING SPILLS WITH HULL DESIGN

NORMAL LOADING

Before Rupture

85'

60'

31.7
pounds per
square inch
(psi)

26.65
psi

After Rupture

Oil
Lost

71.5"

26.65
psi

HYDROSTATIC LOADING

Before Rupture

65'

60'

24.2
psi

26.65
psi

After Rupture

71.5"

54.5'

24.2
psi

24.2
psi

Source: *Scientific American*, October 1991

Tankers can use hydrostatic loading to keep oil from spilling after an accident. With less oil in a hold the oil will exert less pressure than the surrounding seawater, and seawater will flow into a ruptured tank rather than oil flowing out.

During the last 20 years spills the size of the Exxon Valdez *have occurred somewhere in the world's oceans, on average, once each year.*

FOLLOWING THE *Exxon Valdez* oil spill, a number of efforts were made to analyze the causes of the disaster, draw lessons from it, and recommend changes that would lessen the likelihood of similar catastrophes in the future. Subsequently, both Congress and the Alaska Legislature passed new laws governing oil spill prevention and liability, and additional changes have been initiated by the oil industry, U.S. Coast Guard, and others.

Prevention and preparedness are the keys

Every analysis, review, and study of the *Exxon Valdez* spill emphasized the need for stronger preventative measures. Once oil is in the water, only a fraction of it will ever be recovered. Containment and cleanup technology remains primitive, and full repair of environmental damage is beyond human capabilities.

Two areas recognized as having considerable room for improvement were vessel control and ship design. Radar coverage of tanker routes should assure proper monitoring and supervision, navigational aids can be upgraded to provide automatic warnings, and greater use can be made of local pilots and escort vessels. In U.S. waters, the Coast Guard should exert greater authority over vessel movements, with controllers directing and monitoring ships, and areas with specific environmental or economic values or substantial navigational hazards could simply be closed to tanker traffic. Ships built with double hulls would, in most circumstances, limit the amount of oil spilled and slow the rate of discharge. Other design changes, such as protectively located ballast tanks or hydrostatic loading have also been called for. (Hydrostatic loading involves reducing the level of oil in the vessel so that water pressure from outside will push in on and contain the oil in the event of a rupture).

Such preventive measures would go a long way toward preventing the string of human and mechanical errors responsible for

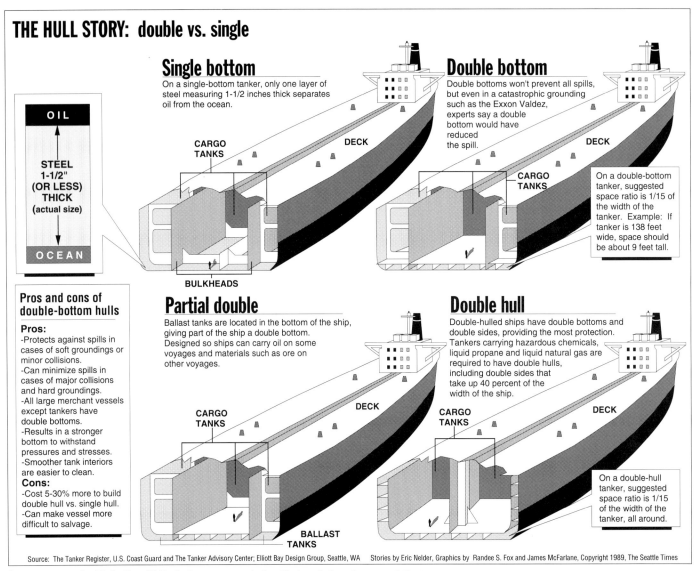

THE HULL STORY: double vs. single

Single bottom

On a single-bottom tanker, only one layer of steel measuring 1-1/2 inches thick separates oil from the ocean.

CARGO TANKS
DECK
BULKHEADS

OIL
STEEL 1-1/2" (OR LESS) THICK (actual size)
OCEAN

Double bottom

Double bottoms won't prevent all spills, but even in a catastrophic grounding such as the Exxon Valdez, experts say a double bottom would have reduced the spill.

CARGO TANKS
DECK

On a double-bottom tanker, suggested space ratio is 1/15 of the width of the tanker. Example: If tanker is 138 feet wide, space should be about 9 feet tall.

Pros and cons of double-bottom hulls

Pros:
- Protects against spills in cases of soft groundings or minor collisions.
- Can minimize spills in cases of major collisions and hard groundings.
- All large merchant vessels except tankers have double bottoms.
- Results in a stronger bottom to withstand pressures and stresses.
- Smoother tank interiors are easier to clean.

Cons:
- Cost 5-30% more to build double hull vs. single hull.
- Can make vessel more difficult to salvage.

Partial double

Ballast tanks are located in the bottom of the ship, giving part of the ship a double bottom. Designed so ships can carry oil on some voyages and materials such as ore on other voyages.

CARGO TANKS
DECK
BALLAST TANKS

Double hull

Double-hulled ships have double bottoms and double sides, providing the most protection. Tankers carrying hazardous chemicals, liquid propane and liquid natural gas are required to have double hulls, including double sides that take up 40 percent of the width of the ship.

CARGO TANKS
DECK

On a double-hull tanker, suggested space ratio is 1/15 of the width of the tanker, all around.

Source: The Tanker Register, U.S. Coast Guard and The Tanker Advisory Center; Elliott Bay Design Group, Seattle, WA   Stories by Eric Nelder, Graphics by Randee S. Fox and James McFarlane, Copyright 1989, The Seattle Times

In most cases, double hulls will limit the amount of oil spilled and slow the rate of discharge. All new tankers built in the U.S. must have double hulls, and existing tankers must be retrofitted or taken out of service by 2010.

the *Exxon Valdez* grounding. Accidents will still happen, however, and responses must be timely and effective. Contingency planning should be just that—detailed blueprints for exact responses to spills of any size, anywhere, under any circumstances. The personnel, equipment, and supplies must always be readily available to implement the plans. Personnel training should involve regular exercises under realistic conditions, with full deployment of equipment. Research and development is needed to secure a more useful arsenal of containment and cleanup technologies. Chemical treatments deserve a great deal more study, as does the practice of bioremediation.

One of the clear lessons from the *Exxon Valdez* spill is that there must be one person immediately in charge of any spill response. This person, who should logically come from the

federal government, should have sole authority and responsibility for nothing other than a successful containment and cleanup. It is neither efficient nor effective to leave the spiller in charge of the cleanup or to have authority divided among a number of players with often-divergent interests.

Changes in law

Very quickly after the spill, Congress and the Alaska Legislature each moved to adopt new—and stricter—legislation designed to better regulate the oil transport industry. Internationally, steps are also being taken through the International Maritime Organization to improve vessel standards and procedures.

The Oil Pollution Act of 1990 (OPA 90), the substance of which

In Prince William Sound navigational controls have been improved by the Coast Guard, and tankers are now accompanied by two escort vessels.

was first proposed in Congress 15 years ago, was finally pushed through as a direct result of outrage over the *Exxon Valdez* spill. Its goals were both to prevent a repeat of such a confused response and to protect against future spills. Under it, the federal government must be prepared to respond to large spills, with primary responsibility resting with the Coast Guard. The act calls for various preventive measures, including training, vessel self-help plans, and double-hulled tankers. Vessel self-help involves providing each tanker with booms, skimmers, and possibly chemical agents to launch a first response to oil it spills. All new tankers built in the U.S. must have double hulls, and existing tankers must be retrofitted with double hulls or taken out of service over the next 20 years.

OPA 90 established a one billion dollar spill response and cleanup fund financed with a nickel-a-barrel fee on both domestic and imported oil. It set up a national center to maintain computerized lists of equipment and personnel, mandated regional depots of cleanup equipment, and increased the liability for shippers for up to $1200 per gross ton spilled. Importantly, it also granted states the right to adopt more stringent regulations.

Another provision of OPA 90 was the creation of regional citizens' advisory councils as independent non-profit organizations to oversee the oil industry. The first two were set up in Alaska —one for Prince William Sound and the other for Cook Inlet. The councils operate under contracts with oil industry organi-

zations, which also fund their activities. The councils have participated in practice spill drills, conducted independent reviews of industry practices, and acted as important links between the citizenry of the regions and the industry that operates there.

Also in 1990, the Alaska Legislature considered several bills similarly aimed at prevention, preparedness, and liability. Alaska adopted increased criminal penalties for the reckless operation of oil carriers and provided for more state monitoring of vessel traffic and inspection of tankers and facilities. The oil industry now is required to have enough equipment stockpiled to respond to spills the size of that of the *Exxon Valdez*, and to have plans to combat even larger spills. The state set up its own nickel-a-barrel fund to pay for equipment and training and established a statewide citizens' oversight council concerned with both oil spills and hazardous substance releases.

These changes in both federal and state law require both funding and strict enforcement to be effective. OPA 90 apparently had little immediate impact. At the end of 1991, the National Contingency Plan mandated by the act was on hold and money had not been appropriated to agencies. The Marine Spill Response Corporation, the industry cooperative formed to establish spill response depots along U.S. coasts, did not plan to cover any of Alaska's waters. A task force set up by the act to audit the trans-Alaska pipeline system for overall safety, integrity and management was never funded or appointed.

On the state level, implementation of oil spill planning regulations was repeatedly delayed, and the final regulations were weakened by intense oil industry lobbying. Money from the nickel-a-barrel fund sat unused; some was spent to hire state employees, but no equipment was purchased or training carried out. Although the budget of Alaska's Department of Environmental Conservation nearly doubled after the spill, many authorized positions went unfilled, and parts of its oil spill program were still not fully implemented more than two years later.

One problem with new liability laws regarding spills is the complaint by tanker owners that their liability is too great—the potential cost so high that they may refuse to enter U.S. waters.

Some industry analysts have suggested that reputable tankers might stay away and leave the U.S. traffic to less responsible "cowboys," which might result in more spills. Under current federal law, oil companies are not responsible for cleanup if the oil they own is spilled while being carried by an independently-owned tanker. Some tanker owners have moved to shield their assets from being seized in the event of a catastrophic spill.

Litigation-driven science

A major concern following the *Exxon Valdez* spill was, in fact, who was liable and for how much damage. Hundreds of civil lawsuits were filed against Exxon by fishermen and others who claimed damage from the spill. Some also sued the State of Alaska for its failure to regulate the oil industry. The state and federal governments charged Exxon with civil complaints and criminal violations.

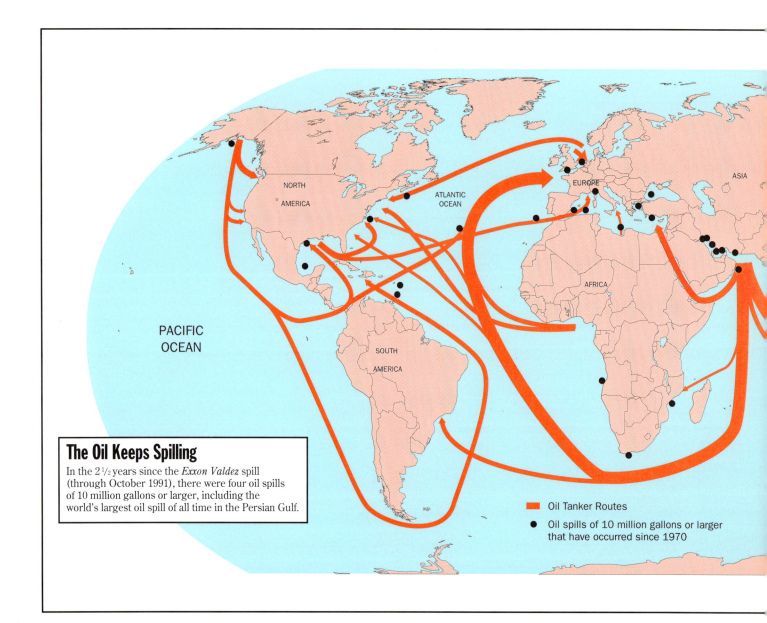

The Oil Keeps Spilling
In the 2½ years since the *Exxon Valdez* spill (through October 1991), there were four oil spills of 10 million gallons or larger, including the world's largest oil spill of all time in the Persian Gulf.

PACIFIC OCEAN

NORTH AMERICA

ATLANTIC OCEAN

EUROPE

ASIA

AFRICA

SOUTH AMERICA

■ Oil Tanker Routes

● Oil spills of 10 million gallons or larger that have occurred since 1970

Both Exxon and the state and federal governments contracted for scientific studies to back their cases. Since the information was expected to be used in court, it was kept secret, not only from the public but within the scientific community, a practice contrary to the normal process of scientific inquiry. A small amount of data was released by the federal government two years after the spill, but the detailed information by which anyone could begin to judge the extent of damages was still being withheld in late 1991. Without knowing the damages, it was difficult to begin to understand the recovery process or to know what treatment or restoration activities were appropriate.

Such secrecy frustrated scientists and the public alike, and raised serious questions about the privatization of science. If science is only conducted and funded by parties with legal and economic stakes in the outcome, how valid can that science be? If it's not reviewed by other experts in the field, is it really science, or is it just data? The scientific community has begun to discuss ways to assure, in the future, that some kind of open exchange can be maintained despite litigation.

Meanwhile, the state and federal governments negotiated a plea bargain with Exxon. Exxon and its shipping subsidiary agreed, in a settlement approved by the courts in October 1991, to plead guilty to misdemeanor violations and to pay one billion dollars. Most of the money will go to a fund that will be spent on restoring damaged resources.

The *Exxon Valdez* oil spill has already been the most-studied major spill to date. However, with the settlement making their court cases moot, the governments' interest in continuing to fund scientific research into long-term effects of the spill is unknown.

Continuing pollution

The *Exxon Valdez* spill was not an isolated event; during the last 20 years spills of its size or larger have occurred somewhere in the world's oceans, on average, once each year. Since the *Exxon Valdez*, the situation has not improved. In fact, in just the first six months of 1991, seven times as much oil was spilled from tankers as in all of 1990, and twice as much as in 1989. Experts say that too many old and poorly maintained vessels with poorly trained crews continue to transport oil from port to port. The 1991 tanker spills have had little press attention in the U.S. because most occurred in foreign waters, often far from shore. Most were due to fires and explosions, which frequently result from structural failures in ships that have not been properly maintained.

While catastrophic spills in sensitive areas capture world

AUSTRALIA

PACIFIC
OCEAN

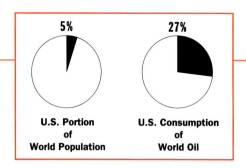

5%

U.S. Portion of World Population

27%

U.S. Consumption of World Oil

attention, chronic oil pollution is considered far more insidious. The two largest sources of oil pollution in the marine environment are still operational discharges from tankers and other vessels and discharges of urban and industrial wastes. Continual releases of even relatively small amounts of oil can seriously harm an ecosystem.

The marine environment does not have an infinite capacity for degradation and detoxification of petroleum compounds, and dilution itself cannot negate their toxic effects. Despite the expanse of the world's oceans, only 10% of their area is considered relevant for food production; it is these same, mostly coastal waters that face today's greatest pollution threats.

In the case of the *Exxon Valdez* spill, much oil remains buried in beach sediments. Beaches that appear clean on the surface typically are found to contain tar deposits under a few inches of gravel. This oil and oil residue, sealed off from oxygen, light, and energy at the surface, is preserved from degradation by sequestration—the same process that has preserved oil within bedrock layers for millions of years. Only as waves turn the gravel and water washes through the beach is the buried oil released. Buried oil that leaks out causes, in effect, a new or continuing spill. The amount of damage it causes will depend on the quality that escapes (how toxic its components are) and the timing and amount of leakage.

U.S. consumption

The United States consumes, mostly by burning, 26–28% of all the oil produced in the world, or 730 million gallons every day. This is two and a half times what the people of Japan and western Europe, per capita, use. Only half of the oil consumed in this country is produced in the U.S., and imports are expected to increase 50% by the year 2000. Most of that oil will be delivered by tankers.

The *Exxon Valdez* disaster awoke Americans to this country's disproportionate consumption of the world's resources, consumption that is at the root of so much pollution and destruction. As one of the most effective post-spill advertisements read, it wasn't Captain Hazelwood's tanker driving that was at fault so much as it was our driving—our generally profligate and inefficient use of fuels in all areas of American life, our throw-away habits that require more and more oil.

In October 1991 Congress turned down an energy bill oriented toward the supply side—more oil production, more nuclear development—rather than the demand side—more conservation. A key feature of the bill would have been the opening of Alaska's Arctic National Wildlife Refuge (ANWR) to oil development. Analysts believe Congress's—and the public's—opposition to the bill was at least partly the legacy of the *Exxon Valdez* spill. More Americans were aware of the environmental costs of energy development and use and were ready to say that some of them were too high. If oil is ever drilled in ANWR, it will be carried to market down the Alaska pipeline and by tankers through Prince William Sound. ■

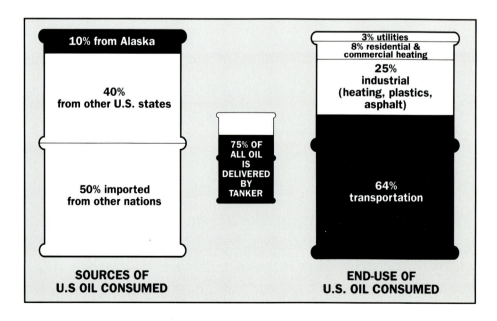

10% from Alaska

40% from other U.S. states

50% imported from other nations

75% OF ALL OIL IS DELIVERED BY TANKER

3% utilities
8% residential & commercial heating

25% industrial (heating, plastics, asphalt)

64% transportation

SOURCES OF U.S OIL CONSUMED

END-USE OF U.S. OIL CONSUMED

Exxon Valdez oil spill

Spill: The Wreck of the Exxon Valdez, Alaska Oil Spill Commission Final Report, State of Alaska, 1990

The Exxon Valdez *Oil Spill: A Management Analysis* by Richard Townsend and Burr Heneman, for Center for Marine Conservation (Washington, D.C.), 1989

In the Wake of the Exxon Valdez: *The Devastating Impact of the Alaska Oil Spill* by Art Davidson, Sierra Club Books (San Francisco), 1990

Out of the Channel: The Exxon Valdez *Oil Spill in Prince William Sound* by John Keeble, HarperCollins (New York), 1991

History—Oil in Alaska

Spill: The Wreck of the Exxon Valdez, p. 29–36

In the Wake of the Exxon Valdez: *The Devastating Impact of the Alaska Oil Spill*, p. xi–xiv and 79–98

Crude Oil in the Sea

Oil in the Sea: Fates, Inputs, and Effects, National Research Council, National Academy Press (Washington, D.C.), 1985

The Control of Oil Pollution edited by J. Wardley-Smith, Graham and Trotman Limited (London), 1983

Out of the Channel: The Exxon Valdez *Oil Spill in Prince William Sound*, p. 195–206

Oil in the Food Web—Biological Effects

Oil in the Sea: Fates, Inputs, and Effects

"Impact on Human Health of Petroleum in the Marine Environment" by Ieva Politzer, Ildefonso DeLeon, and John Laseter for American Petroleum Institute (Washington, D.C.), 1985

"Summary of Effects of the *Exxon Valdez* Oil Spill on Natural Resources and Archaeological Resources," document released by U.S. Departments of Interior and Agriculture and the National Oceanic and Atmospheric Adminstration, March 1991

Native Subsistence

"Patterns of Wild Resource Use in English Bay and Port Graham, Alaska" by Ronald T. Stanek, technical paper no. 104, Division of Subsistence, Alaska Department of Fish and Game (Anchorage, Alaska), 1985

"Resource Use Patterns in Chenega, Western Prince William Sound: Chenega in the 1960s and Chenega Bay 1984–1986" by Lee Stratton and Evelyn B. Chisum, technical paper no. 139, Division of Subsistence, Alaska Department of Fish and Game (Anchorage, Alaska), 1986

"Subsistence Uses of Fish and Wildlife and the *Exxon Valdez* Oil Spill," by James Fall in Arctic Issues Digest, University of Alaska Cooperative Extension Service (Anchorage, Alaska), 1991

Cleanup

The Control of Oil Pollution

Coping with an Oiled Sea: An Analysis of Oil Spill Response Technologies, background paper OTA-BP-0-63, U.S. Congress Office of Technology Assessment, March 1990

"Soiled Shores" by Marguerite Holloway, Scientific American, October 1991

Animal Rescue and Rehabilitation

The Exxon Valdez *Oil Spill: A Management Analysis*, p. 98–129

Sea Otter Symposium: Proceedings of a Symposium to Evaluate the Response Effort on Behalf of Sea Otters After the T/V Exxon Valdez *Oil Spill Into Prince William Sound* coordinated and edited by Keith Bayha and Jennifer Kormendy, U.S. Fish and Wildlife Service, biological report 90(12), 1990

"Terror and Triage at the Laundry" by Jon R. Luoma, Audubon, September 1989

Recovery and Restoration

Restoration of Habitats Impacted by Oil Spills edited by John Cairns, Jr. and Arthur L. Buikema, Jr., An Ann Arbor Science Book, Butterworth Publishers (Boston), 1984

Restoration Planning Following the Exxon Valdez *Oil Spill: August 1990 Progress Report* prepared by the Restoration Planning Work Group (Alaska Departments of Fish and Game, Natural Resources, and Environmental Conservation; U.S. Departments of Agriculture, Commerce, and Interior: and the U.S. Environmental Protection Agency

Will It Happen Again?

Spill: The Wreck of the Exxon Valdez

The Exxon Valdez *Oil Spill: A Management Analysis*

Oil Spill Intelligence Report, an international weekly newsletter from Cutter Information Corp. (Massachusetts)

CREDITS/ACKNOWLEDGMENTS

This publication was made possible through the generous support of the National Science Foundation. Opinions expressed are those of the author and not necessarily those of the Foundation.

PRATT MUSEUM STAFF

Betsy Pitzman, *Director*

Martha Madsen, *Curator of Education*

Mike O'Meara, *Guest Curator*

Publication Reviewers/Advisors

Alan Boraas
Richard Brusca
Steve Bugbee
Tom Kizzia
Walt Parker
George C. West

Publication Photographers
Al Allen
Randy Brandon
Eberhard Brunner
Alissa Crandall
Norma Wolf Dudiak
Patrick Endres
Natalie Fobes
Greg Gilbert, *Seattle Times*
Ken Graham Photography
Eric Gundlach
Bob Hallinen, *Anchorage Daily News*
John Hyde, Alaska Department of
　Fish and Game
Karen Jettmar
John S. Lough, Wilderness Exposure
Terrence McCarthy
Nancy Menning, Environmental
　Protection Agency
Charles Gil Mull
Lisa Scarbrough, Alaska Department of
　Fish and Game
Ron Staneck, Alaska Department of
　Fish and Game
Harold E. Wilson

Exhibit Developer and Manager
Kathleen McLean, Independent Exhibitions

Exhibit Designer
Gordon Chun Design

Exhibit Fabricator
Jonathan Hirabayashi Design

Exhibit Advisory Committee

Poppy L. Benson
Outdoor Recreation Planner
U.S. Fish and Wildlife Service

Alan Boraas, Ph.D.
Associate Professor of Anthropology
Kenai Peninsula College

Richard C. Brusca, Ph.D.
Department of Marine Invertebrates
San Diego Natural History Museum

Billy Choate
Native Alaskan (Inupiat)
Commerical Fisherman

William B. Driskell
Marine Biology Consultant
Seattle, Washington

Charles Konigsberg, Ph.D.
Professor of Political Science, retired
Alaska Pacific University

Dennis C. Lees
Marine Ecology Consultant
E.R.C. Environmental

Craig Matkin, M.S.
Marine Mammals Biologist
North Gulf Coast Oceanic Society

Susan C. Matthews, M.S.
Wildlife Education Specialist
U.S. Fish and Wildlife Service

Janet Pawlukiewicz, M.A.
Outreach Coordinator
U.S. Environmental Protection Agency

Lee Post
Pratt Museum Volunteer and Naturalist

Jack Sobel
Director of Habitat Conservation
Center for Marine Conservation

Paul Schmidt
Deputy Assistant Regional Director
U.S. Fish and Wildlife Service,
Alaska Region

George C. West, Ph.D.
Professor of Zoophysiology, Emeritus
University of Alaska Fairbanks

Exhibit Contributors

Alaska Conservation Foundation
Alaska Department of Environmental
　Conservation
Alaska Department of Fish and Game
Alaska Department of Natural Resources
Alaska Humanities Forum, an affiliate of the
　National Endowment for the Humanities
Anchorage Audubon Society
Baha'i Community of Homer
Center for Alaskan Coastal Studies
Center for Marine Conservation
Environmental Protection Agency
Willie and Karen Flyum/Dolphin Leasing, Inc.
International Fund for Animal Welfare
National Audubon Society
National Fish and Wildlife Foundation
National Park Service, Alaska Region
National Science Foundation
National Wildlife Federation
Office of Ocean Resources Conservation and
　Assessment, NOAA
Oil Spill Intelligence Report
Recreation Equipment, Inc.
Regional Citizens Advisory Council
Seventh Generation, Inc.
State-Federal Restoration Planning Work Group
Town Creek Foundation
True North Foundation
U.S. Fish and Wildlife Service, Alaska Region
Wynn Foundation